THE FORGOTTEN LAWS OF MANIFESTATION

By Aria Vale

Copyright © 2025 Aria Vale
All rights reserved.

No part of this book may be reproduced, distributed, or transmitted in any form or by any means, including photocopying, recording, or other electronic or mechanical methods, without the prior written permission of the author, except in the case of brief quotations used in critical reviews and certain other noncommercial uses permitted by copyright law.

Introduction – Why Most People Fail to Manifest Even When They Believe
by Aria Vale

For years, people have been told that they can "manifest anything." The message is simple: *just think positive, visualize it, and believe.* Millions have repeated affirmations in the mirror, written goals in journals, and waited for their dreams to arrive. Yet most of them are still stuck broke, anxious, and wondering why nothing seems to work.

They've been told they're the problem. That their "vibration" isn't high enough. That they didn't believe hard enough. That if they just kept pretending to be happy, life would eventually reward them. But the truth is harder to swallow: the system they've been sold is broken. It's not that people failed to manifest it's that they were taught a counterfeit version of manifestation.

Modern self-help has turned spiritual truth into a marketing product. It preaches ease without effort, reward without discipline, and blessings without obedience. It promises miracles for the price of a course. It tells people that they are their own gods, that reality bends to their desires, and that faith is simply "energy." Yet that message is empty. It feeds the ego, not the soul.

This is why so many people read endless books, attend seminars, and feel inspired for a week but soon fall back into fear, doubt, and apathy. Because motivation fades. Emotion burns out. And without divine order, there's no structure to sustain what they seek.

True manifestation is not about demanding reality to give you what you want. It's about aligning yourself with the principles God already designed laws that govern creation, order, growth, and blessing. These laws are not secret, mystical, or hidden behind rituals. They are written in both Scripture and science. But they've been *forgotten* in a world that worships shortcuts and emotion instead of truth.

The Illusion of Effortless Power

The rise of "manifestation gurus" has created a generation that believes feelings create facts. They teach people to focus only on what feels good, to avoid discomfort, and to expect instant results. But anything worth having requires growth and growth always demands struggle. You can't build strength without resistance. You can't develop faith without testing. You can't expect harvest without planting, watering, and waiting.

When people are told manifestation should be effortless, they begin to resent the process. The moment life gets hard, they assume something's wrong. They quit, thinking they've failed when in truth, that difficulty was the exact step they needed to take.

The real problem isn't that people don't believe. It's that they believe in a distorted version of belief — one divorced from truth, responsibility, and obedience. Faith without works is dead, and manifestation without discipline is illusion.

God's system isn't built to cater to ego; it's built to refine it. Every true manifestation aligns with His laws: patience, order, stewardship, persistence, gratitude, and moral integrity. These are the *forgotten laws* — the ones self-help doesn't sell because they require sacrifice.

The Crisis of Shallow Spirituality

There's a reason why so many people are spiritually exhausted. They've tried to fill their emptiness with affirmations instead of alignment. They've treated God like a vending machine — insert belief, receive miracle. But faith doesn't operate on demand. Faith transforms the believer before it transforms their circumstances.

The modern world sells instant gratification, but the spiritual world operates on cultivation. Just as a farmer must plant before harvest, so must the human mind be renewed before results appear. But this isn't the message that sells. The real message — that transformation requires discipline, humility, and surrender — is too difficult for the masses, so it's replaced with easier slogans:
"You can have it all."

"You are the universe."
"Just manifest it."

The result? People who confuse emotional highs for spiritual awakening. They chase motivation, not mastery. They accumulate "knowledge" but never apply it. They manifest nothing because they never matured enough to handle what they asked for.

Manifestation is not magic. It's divine alignment. It's not a formula for control but a process of surrender not to the world, but to the higher order of God's principles.

The Forgotten Truth

When I began my own journey, I was obsessed with finding the "secret." I read hundreds of books. I experimented with every technique scripting, visualization, vision boards, frequency meditations, affirmations. Some things worked, most didn't. I'd experience temporary results, only to fall back into doubt.

It wasn't until I stopped chasing and started submitting that I saw the pattern. Every "law" I tested that worked was already written in Scripture though the wording was different. The history had already explained the mechanics: sowing and reaping, faith and action, stewardship, gratitude, perseverance, patience, obedience, and renewal of the mind. The very laws that modern gurus "rebranded" were never theirs to begin with.

I realized manifestation isn't about *creating your own truth* it's about aligning with *the truth that already exists*. When you walk in harmony with God's order, your desires evolve to match your purpose. You stop chasing temporary outcomes and start creating eternal impact.

The "forgotten laws" are not mystical teachings. They are divine systems psychological, spiritual, and biological that govern how faith becomes form. When your mind, emotions, and actions align with these laws, manifestation becomes a byproduct of obedience, not manipulation.

What This Book Will Teach You

This book is not a motivational pep talk. It is a wake-up call.

It will expose how modern manifestation teachings have replaced truth with trends. It will dismantle the illusion that you can "attract" what you're unwilling to embody. It will show you why affirmations without alignment lead to emptiness, and why faith without discipline collapses under pressure.

You will learn that:

- Manifestation requires stewardship you must manage what you already have before receiving more.
- Faith must be tested and every delay or obstacle is part of that test.
- Thoughts matter, but only when they are consistent with godly action.
- Emotion is energy, but without structure it becomes chaos.
- Vision requires pruning not everything you want is meant for you.
- Gratitude is not a mindset trick it's the language of divine trust.
- Prayer is not begging it's alignment.
- And miracles are never random they are results of obedience to divine laws.

Each chapter of this book reveals one of these forgotten laws the foundational principles that connect psychology, neuroscience, and biblical truth. You will not find empty promises or mystical jargon here. Instead, you will find practical spiritual discipline rooted in logic and faith.

You will see how your brain responds to belief, how consistency rewires neural pathways, how faith sharpens focus, and how obedience activates unseen doors. Science and Scripture, when read together, reveal the same pattern: transformation begins from within and manifests outward.

A Higher Calling

You were not made to live small. But the path to expansion is narrow. True manifestation doesn't inflate ego it humbles it. It doesn't glorify you it glorifies the One who created you. When you align with God's laws, your life reflects divine order: clarity replaces confusion, peace replaces anxiety, and purpose replaces emptiness.

This is not a promise of an easy life. It's a promise of a meaningful one. The forgotten laws demand faith when evidence is absent, patience when timing feels unfair, and persistence when the world gives up. But they also deliver results that no man can take credit for because they're built on God's foundation, not man's manipulation.

So if you're ready to stop chasing illusions, to rebuild your faith on truth instead of trends, and to finally manifest in alignment with divine order this book will guide you.

You don't need to become more "positive." You need to become more *aligned*.
You don't need to fake belief. You need to act on faith.

You don't need another technique. You need the truth.

Welcome to *The Forgotten Laws of Manifestation*.

Reflection / Action Step:
Pause before continuing. Reflect honestly: Have you been manifesting from ego or from obedience? Write down one belief you've accepted from modern self-help that now feels false. Replace it with this truth: *"Manifestation is not about getting what I want it's about becoming who God created me to be."*

Contents

Chapter 1 – The Lie of Effortless Manifestation 13

Chapter 2 – The Law of Aligned Action 22

Chapter 3 – The Law of Stewardship 31

Chapter 4 – The Biology of Belief 41

Chapter 5 – The Frequency of Thought: How the Brain Emits Reality 51

Chapter 6 – The Architecture of Time: Why Manifestation Requires Delay 62

Chapter 7 – The Human Mirror: Stories of Faith in Motion 73

Chapter 8 – The Law of Resistance: Why Opposition Is Proof of Alignment 82

Chapter 9 – The Law of Rest: The Silence After Alignment 92

Chapter 10 – The Law of the Hidden Order: How Chaos Conceals Precision 102

Chapter 11 – The Law of the Silent Signal: How Subconscious Frequencies Speak Louder Than Words 113

Chapter 12 – The Law of Collapse: The Fall Before Freedom 124

Chapter 13 – The Law of the Hollow World: How Modern Life Kills the Soul 131

Chapter 14 – The Law of Withdrawal: The Power of Disappearing from the System 138

Chapter 15 – The Law of the Inner Architecture: How Thought Becomes Structure 146

Chapter 16 – The Law of Friction: Make the Right Thing Inevitable 154

Chapter 17 – The Law of Systems: You Don't Rise to Goals, You Fall to Design 161

Chapter 18 – The Law of Integration: When All Systems Converge 168

Chapter 19 – The Law of Perception Collapse: When Reality Stops Being Objective 175

Chapter 20 – The Law of Continuum: Why Evolution Never Ends 182

Conclusion – The Return to Origin 187

Chapter 1 – The Lie of Effortless Manifestation

by Aria Vale

For decades, people have been sold a comfortable illusion that manifestation is effortless. That if you think the right thoughts, feel "high vibration," and visualize hard enough, reality will hand you everything you want. It sounds beautiful. It feels empowering. But it is a lie.

This belief has quietly destroyed more potential than failure ever could. Because failure teaches. Illusion sedates. The idea of effortless manifestation doesn't liberate people it paralyzes them. It turns potential creators into passive dreamers, waiting for life to move without ever learning how to move with it.

The Seduction of Ease

The modern self-help industry discovered something dangerous: people buy comfort more eagerly than truth. So it built a gospel of ease "You don't need to work hard, you just need to believe." The message spread quickly because it fed the two things the ego craves most: validation and control.

It told people that emotions alone shape reality, that struggle is unnecessary, that discipline is obsolete.

Principles once considered essential — patience, integrity, endurance, and service — were rebranded as "low vibration." The modern seeker became addicted to comfort disguised as spirituality.

The deception is subtle. It doesn't reject effort; it redefines it. It tells you that feeling good *is* the work. That raising your vibration through playlists, journaling, or affirmations replaces deliberate movement. But no amount of positive emotion can substitute for consistency, structure, or follow-through.

The result is a generation of people who can describe their dream life in vivid detail — yet remain stuck, anxious, and spiritually fatigued. While their minds were busy imagining, their hands never built.

The Psychology of False Productivity

This culture of effortless manifestation thrives because it hijacks the brain's reward circuitry. When you visualize your dream or repeat affirmations, your brain releases small hits of dopamine — the same neurochemical that fuels scrolling and gambling.

You feel productive without doing anything. The brain confuses fantasy for progress. This forms a loop: the more you imagine, the more chemically "rewarded" you feel and the less urgency you have to act.

Eventually, discipline atrophies. You start believing that taking real steps will "interfere with the flow." So you wait. You keep "aligning your energy." You buy new courses, new tools, new reasons to delay. But readiness never arrives because readiness is built through motion, not meditation.

Manifestation requires movement. Transformation demands effort. Even in nature, every birth begins with labor. Every breakthrough follows preparation. Action precedes confirmation.

Modern spirituality has replaced movement with mood. It tells you to sit still and trust that things will unfold and when they don't, it blames you. Your "energy." Your "resistance." The cycle continues: self-blame, false hope, another course, another high.

The Comfort of Spiritual Laziness

The promise of effortless creation flatters human weakness. It whispers, "You are powerful; you don't need to struggle. Just think it into being." It transforms discipline into self-indulgence.

It's appealing because it removes accountability. If everything depends on your "vibration," then perseverance, consistency, and moral responsibility no longer matter. You can ignore your duties and call it surrender. You can avoid challenge and name it faith.

But genuine growth isn't designed to be comfortable. The laws of existence don't reward ease; they reward alignment through effort. Every form of mastery physical, mental, or creative demands confrontation with resistance.

The illusion of effortless manifestation collapses under pressure. When difficulty appears, people trained in ease interpret it as failure. They mistake discomfort for misalignment, never realizing that friction is the forge of growth. Challenge doesn't block the path it *is* the path.

The Trap of Selective Trust

One of the most damaging consequences of this mindset is selective trust believing only when it feels good.

Imagine a person who dreams of starting a business. Each morning, she repeats affirmations: *I am abundant. Money flows easily to me.* She fills her walls with vision boards. One day, a colleague offers her a real opportunity but it demands long hours, uncertainty, and courage. She declines, saying, "If it's meant to be, it will come effortlessly."

Months pass. Nothing changes. She grows bitter, wondering why her affirmations "failed." But they didn't. The opportunity appeared she just refused the version that required evolution. She wanted instant reward, not partnership with reality.

Trust without motion is avoidance. Belief without follow-through is fantasy.

If you truly believe something is possible, your behavior reflects it. Conviction expresses itself through movement. To wait endlessly for the "perfect sign" is to mistake comfort for clarity.

The Discipline of Real Manifestation

True manifestation is not about attraction it's about transformation. It asks for self-mastery: disciplined thought, emotional regulation, and the endurance to act without visible proof.

Most people quit here. They confuse natural resistance with cosmic rejection. They think the universe is withholding, when in truth, it is preparing. Real manifestation takes time because it develops the strength required to hold what you ask for.

The self-help market sells inspiration; universal order builds endurance. Inspiration fades quickly. Endurance matures into stability. Manifestations achieved without effort dissolve just as easily because the structure behind them was never strong enough to sustain weight.

Every discipline follows the same law: repetition compounds. You cannot rewire your mind through imagination alone it requires consistent correction. You cannot align with higher order while ignoring the demands of reality.

Manifestation isn't control. It's collaboration with the architecture of cause and effect.

The Difference Between Faith and Fantasy

Faith in life, in universal order, in potential operates within reality. It acknowledges uncertainty and still acts. Fantasy avoids it.

When people say, "I'll just trust the universe," they often mean, "I don't want to face the discomfort of effort." But no intelligent system rewards inertia. The laws that govern creation require participation.

History honors those who moved before assurance explorers who sailed beyond maps, inventors who built without proof, thinkers who worked through ridicule. They didn't manifest by wishing; they acted by conviction.

Modern manifestation culture mimics faith but removes accountability. It wants results without refinement, rewards without reform. But universal law responds to coherence, not comfort. It rewards courage, discipline, and integrity.

Reclaiming the Forgotten Standard

Effort is not the enemy of creation it is its proof. Every genuine act of alignment requires cost. You release excuses. You trade emotion for execution. You sacrifice ease for evolution.

This is not about forcing outcomes. It's about cooperating with order becoming the kind of person whose actions match their intentions.

When you move decisively, effort becomes a signal a declaration that you trust the process more than your comfort. That's when things begin to align. Because movement affirms belief far more powerfully than words ever could.

Manifestation, in its truest form, is partnership with the higher structure that governs all things. It's not about commanding life it's about learning to live in rhythm with its design.

Reflection / Action Step

Ask yourself: Have I been trying to manifest from comfort instead of commitment?

Write down one area of your life where you've been waiting for change to arrive on its own. Then list one concrete action however small that demonstrates your belief in progress.

Remember: conviction isn't measured by what you *say* you believe, but by what you're willing to do when belief is tested.

Take one deliberate step.
Not because you're forcing life to obey but because you trust that the structure of life rewards movement, not passivity.

Chapter 2 – The Law of Aligned Action

by Aria Vale

Manifestation begins in the mind, but it becomes real only through motion. Thought creates direction; faith fuels persistence; action gives it form. Without action, belief is just imagination. God's system blesses alignment when mind, spirit, and behavior move as one toward truth.

Wishful Thinking vs. Faithful Doing

There is a profound difference between wishful thinking and faithful doing. Wishful thinking hopes something will happen *to* you. Faithful doing moves as if it's already possible *through* you. Wishful thinkers wait for signs, timing, or luck. Faithful doers act while trusting God to meet them in the process.

The modern world glorifies visualization but neglects obedience. It celebrates "manifesting" but forgets the command to "walk by faith." Real manifestation doesn't occur when you talk about what you want; it begins when your steps reflect what you believe.

Every miracle in Scripture follows this pattern. When Jesus healed the man with the withered hand, He didn't simply declare it healed. He said, *"Stretch out your hand."* When the lepers cried for mercy, He said, *"Go show yourselves to the priests,"* and *as they went,* they were cleansed. The power moved *through* their obedience, not before it.

Faith is not pretending the road is clear. Faith is walking even when the road is foggy, trusting that every step you take in truth will reveal the next one.

The Physics of Alignment

Alignment means your thoughts, words, and behavior point in the same direction. When your mind prays for one thing but your actions contradict it, you create internal chaos. You say you trust God for provision, yet you never manage your money. You say you're believing for better health, but you treat your body carelessly. You say you want purpose, but you refuse to leave your comfort zone.

This double-mindedness is why progress stalls. Old spiritual texts, *"A double-minded man is unstable in all his ways."* Manifestation requires internal unity not perfection, but direction. The moment your actions begin to mirror your convictions, your energy, focus, and opportunities align like gears in motion.

In neuroscience, this is called **cognitive consistency.** The brain naturally seeks harmony between belief and behavior. When they don't match, it triggers dissonance an inner tension that drains motivation. But when they do match, the brain releases dopamine and strengthens neural pathways associated with confidence and reward. Every small, aligned action literally rewires your mind to expect success, because it proves that belief and effort are synchronized.

How Action Strengthens Faith

Faith doesn't grow from waiting; it grows from movement. When you act despite uncertainty, your brain collects evidence that your trust is justified. This process builds a feedback loop between belief and behavior. Each act of courage reinforces your conviction, and that conviction fuels stronger action.

This is why God rarely gives people the full picture. He gives instruction, not guarantees. If you obey, the next step appears. The longer you hesitate, the quieter His guidance feels not because He withdraws, but because faith grows only in motion.

When Joshua faced the walls of Jericho, God could have flattened them instantly. Instead, He told Joshua to march around them for seven days. It seemed illogical, even embarrassing. But obedience in small, consistent steps prepared the people's hearts for victory. The walls didn't fall because of sound they fell because of spiritual alignment between faith and action.

The Paralysis of Overthinking

Many people confuse analysis with faith. They wait to feel "certain" before they move. But faith begins where certainty ends. Overthinking is the mind's attempt to replace trust with control. It sounds wise, but it's fear disguised as intelligence.

The person who spends years "planning" but never acting is often more trapped than the one who risks and fails. Because even failure produces momentum. Motion creates feedback, correction, and clarity. Stagnation only breeds confusion.

If you've ever felt "stuck," it's rarely because God withheld something. It's because you stopped moving. God steers moving ships, not anchored ones. You don't need the whole map to take the first step just enough light for the next one.

A Real Story of Aligned Action

Maria, a young woman I once coached, spent years saying she wanted to change her career. She believed God had something greater for her than her repetitive office job. Every morning she journaled, prayed, and visualized her dream life. But she never applied for a single position or took a single class.

One day, she confessed that she felt spiritually disconnected. "I'm doing everything," she said, "but nothing changes." I asked her one question: *"What action today reflects the faith you claim to have?"*

That question broke something in her. She realized she had been waiting for a sign instead of becoming one. That week, she took a small, imperfect step she signed up for a design course. Within months, she built a portfolio and applied for a creative job. The first company rejected her, the second never replied, but the third offered her a position that eventually turned into her dream career.

When she looked back, she told me, "It all started the moment I stopped waiting for alignment and became aligned."

The Biology of Faithful Behavior

From a neuroscience perspective, every action you repeat strengthens a network of neurons called a **habit loop.** The more you act in alignment with your vision, the more your brain encodes that identity as normal. This is how transformation happens not through sudden revelation, but through repetition.

If you say, "I'm a disciplined person," but never act disciplined, the brain dismisses the statement as false. But if you consistently behave like one waking early, focusing, following through those neural pathways grow thicker, faster, and more automatic. You literally become what you repeatedly do.

This is why Scripture emphasizes obedience. God designed the brain to reflect the spirit's choices. When you act in faith, you are not just changing circumstances you're rewiring the biology of belief.

God Blesses Movement

Divine power responds to motion, not apathy. When the Israelites stood before the Red Sea, Moses cried out in fear. God didn't say, "Keep praying." He said, *"Why do you cry to Me? Tell the people to go forward."* Only when they moved did the sea part.

Movement is the language of faith. Every step you take toward obedience tells heaven, *"I trust You more than my fear."* And in that trust, unseen forces begin to cooperate doors open, people appear, strength multiplies.

Waiting becomes holy only when it's *active waiting* when you're preparing, improving, and obeying in expectation. Passive waiting, however, kills faith. It convinces you that delay is spiritual when it's really avoidance.

The Subtle Power of Small Steps

Big breakthroughs are built from small, faithful steps. One aligned action carries more power than a hundred affirmations. Consistency transforms identity because it proves to your own mind that you mean what you say.

Each day you act in alignment, your mind becomes quieter, your focus sharper, and your inner resistance weaker. You stop asking, "Will this work?" and start asking, "How can I serve through it?" That shift marks the beginning of true manifestation not when you get what you want, but when you become the person ready to receive it.

The Weight of Responsibility

Manifestation is not magic; it's responsibility. When you pray for more, God tests whether you can manage what you already have. If you can't steward a small task with excellence, why would He entrust you with greater influence?

Aligned action proves maturity. It shows that your faith is not emotional, but operational. You no longer need the thrill of hope to move; you move because obedience is its own reward.

This maturity is what separates dreamers from doers. Dreamers rely on motivation; doers rely on discipline. Dreamers chase timing; doers create it. Dreamers wait for conditions; doers shape them through persistence and faith.

The Ripple Effect of Alignment

When you act in faith, your behavior influences everything around you. Your energy changes. Your words carry conviction. People notice your consistency and begin to trust your leadership. Opportunities arise because aligned people are predictable in the best way   dependable, grounded, and focused.

God honors this. His system is built on order. He doesn't reward empty belief but faithful execution. The law of aligned action operates quietly but relentlessly: what you sow through consistent faith, you will eventually reap through divine timing.

Reflection / Action Step

Ask yourself: *Where does my faith stop and my hesitation begin?* Identify one area of your life where your prayers and your habits contradict. Write it down honestly. Then choose one small, visible action that aligns with the belief you claim to have.

Do it today not tomorrow. Momentum is built by movement, not intention. Remember: God multiplies direction, not indecision. When you move in alignment with faith, heaven meets you halfway.

CHAPTER 2
THE LAW OF ALIGNED ACTION
by Aria Vale

Chapter 3 – The Law of Stewardship
by Aria Vale

Manifestation does not begin when you ask for more. It begins when you take responsibility for what you already have. Every blessing in God's system multiplies through stewardship the careful, disciplined management of what has already been placed in your hands.

Many people believe they're being "tested by delay," when in reality, they are being *tested by management.* They cry for greater opportunities, higher income, deeper relationships, and stronger purpose, yet the soil of their daily life remains unattended. Unpaid bills, wasted hours, unresolved conflict, and ignored responsibilities quietly block the very increase they pray for.

God does not reward begging. He rewards partnership. And partnership begins with stewardship.

Faithfulness Precedes Increase

Scripture states, *"He who is faithful with little will be entrusted with much."* It's not a metaphor it's a spiritual law. God never multiplies chaos. He multiplies order. If He gave you more while you still mismanage what you have, the blessing would collapse under its own weight.

A person who mishandles $100 will mishandle $10,000. A person who can't manage one hour with focus will waste ten. The principle doesn't change with scale only the consequences grow.

We often say we're ready for "the next level," but readiness isn't measured by desire. It's measured by discipline. God measures faith not by what you *wish* to do, but by how you handle what's already in front of you.

The Deception of Wanting "More"

Modern culture glorifies expansion bigger goals, more followers, more possessions. People chase quantity, believing it will fix the emptiness created by lack of quality. But expansion without structure breeds anxiety, not abundance.

The person who prays for more money but ignores budgeting is not asking for provision they're asking for permission to continue being careless. The person who asks for a better relationship but refuses to communicate with respect is not seeking love they're seeking validation.

Manifestation doesn't magnify who you wish to be. It magnifies who you already are. If your foundation is unstable, increase will expose it. If your habits are inconsistent, success will break them. That's why God waits not because He's withholding, but because He's protecting.

When you learn to manage little things with care, you prove to heaven that you can be trusted with greater weight. Stewardship is preparation disguised as responsibility.

A Practical Story: The Lesson of the Ledger

Marcus, a man in his thirties, once told me he had been praying for financial breakthrough for years. He tithed occasionally, repeated affirmations about wealth, and even wrote on his mirror, *"I am a millionaire in the making."* Yet every month ended the same stress, debt, and confusion.

One day, he confessed that he felt abandoned by God. "I'm doing everything right," he said. "I'm visualizing abundance. Why am I still broke?"

I asked a simple question: "Do you know where your money goes each month?"

He hesitated. "Not exactly."

I handed him a small notebook and said, "For the next 30 days, write down every dollar you spend every coffee, subscription, and impulse buy. Don't judge it. Just track it."

At first, he resisted. It felt tedious. But within two weeks, he saw the truth: over a quarter of his income was vanishing on distractions. Streaming services, late fees, takeout meals. He realized his lack wasn't spiritual it was managerial.

That month, he canceled what he didn't need, set aside 10% for savings, and began tithing consistently. Within three months, he landed a new client through a referral that came from someone he'd helped years earlier an opportunity that had always existed but was invisible to him until his mind became clear.

When I asked what changed, he said, "Nothing outside me I just started honoring what I already had."

That is the essence of stewardship: honor births multiplication.

Gratitude and Order: Two Sides of the Same Law

Gratitude and stewardship are inseparable. Gratitude is the emotion of faith; stewardship is its expression. Gratitude without responsibility is sentiment. Stewardship without gratitude becomes duty. Together, they create alignment.

When you truly value something, you protect it. You maintain it. You organize it. Gratitude makes you attentive; attention multiplies value. Whether it's your health, your home, your relationships, or your work whatever you appreciate grows stronger under care.

Psychology supports this truth. When you organize your environment, track your habits, and bring order to small details, your brain's **prefrontal cortex** the area responsible for focus and planning becomes more active. This leads to greater clarity, emotional regulation, and creativity.

The simple act of managing what's yours rewires your brain toward abundance. You stop reacting and start directing. You move from survival to stewardship.

The Neuroscience of Responsibility

In neuroscience, there's a principle known as **attentional control.** What you consistently focus on becomes your brain's priority. When your attention is scattered, your life follows. But when you focus on improving what you already have even in small ways your brain encodes that pattern as safety and growth.

The more you manage, the more capacity you build. As neural pathways strengthen through repeated responsible behavior, your tolerance for complexity increases. This is why organized people often attract more opportunities   not by luck, but because their nervous system is structured for expansion.

Disorder signals the brain that you're already at capacity. That's why cluttered minds and chaotic spaces block inspiration. Stewardship is not just spiritual obedience; it's neurological optimization. It creates the mental space where new blessings can land without overwhelming you.

God's System Rewards Responsibility

God's design for increase is not arbitrary. He blesses those who manage, not those who merely ask. Prayer without stewardship is like planting seeds and refusing to water them. The soil is fertile, but the gardener is asleep.

The parable of the talents in Matthew 25 illustrates this perfectly. Three servants receive resources from their master. Two invest and multiply what they were given. The third buries his portion in fear. When the master returns, he rewards the first two, saying, *"Well done, good and faithful servant. You have been faithful over a few things; I will make you ruler over many."* But to the third, he says, *"You wicked and lazy servant."*

Notice the contrast: the faithful were promoted because they managed; the fearful were demoted because they avoided. God didn't punish the third servant for failure He corrected him for passivity. The same law applies today: increase is the reward of stewardship, not emotion.

The Hidden Cost of Neglect

Neglect is not neutral it's corrosive. What you ignore decays. Relationships drift, finances leak, health deteriorates, opportunities expire. Yet neglect often disguises itself as "waiting on timing." People tell themselves, *"When I have more, I'll manage better."* But the truth is the opposite: you get more *because* you manage better.

Every neglected area drains spiritual authority. When you avoid small responsibilities, your confidence erodes. The mind senses disorder and mirrors it through anxiety and confusion. This is why so many feel "stuck" even when they're praying they are asking for progress while tolerating disorder.

Manifestation doesn't require perfection; it requires attention. Start by tending to one neglected corner of your life, and you'll feel the shift immediately. The moment you bring order, peace returns.

The Spiritual Weight of Care

To steward something is to reflect God's character because God Himself is a steward. The entire universe operates through order: seasons, cycles, and systems. When you live in alignment with that order, you participate in creation instead of resisting it.

Every resource you've been given your body, time, talents, and influence is on loan. Stewardship is not ownership; it's partnership. You manage what belongs to God. When you care for it diligently, He trusts you with more.

This law doesn't just govern money. It applies to your health, your emotions, your relationships, and your time. How you treat each area reflects how much you value the One who gave it. Neglect reveals disbelief. Care reveals faith.

From Scarcity to Multiplication

Scarcity is not the absence of resources it's the absence of stewardship. When people manage poorly, they live in cycles of waste and wonder why nothing multiplies. But the moment they shift from consumption to cultivation, everything changes.

Think of a garden. You can't demand fruit from soil you refuse to till. God's blessings are seeds they require work, patience, and maintenance. But when you tend to them faithfully, they multiply beyond expectation.

Abundance is not the miracle. Stewardship is the miracle that makes abundance sustainable.

Reflection / Action Step

Examine your life honestly. Which area have you been neglecting while praying for more? Money, health, relationships, purpose, or time?

Choose one and begin managing it with excellence not to earn blessing, but to align with it. Create a simple plan: track, organize, and care for what's already in your hands.

Say this aloud: *"I will no longer ask for more while ignoring what I have. I will honor what's mine as an act of faith."*

The moment you do, you'll feel the current shift because stewardship isn't just management. It's manifestation in motion.

Chapter 4 – The Biology of Belief

by Aria Vale

For centuries, belief was treated as something mystical an invisible force shaping life through unseen energy. But belief is not a mystery floating in the clouds; it is biology in motion. Faith is not only spiritual it is physiological. Every conviction you hold, every expectation you repeat, leaves a measurable imprint on your brain, your hormones, and your behavior.

The unseen world of the mind is not made of vapor; it is made of neurons, chemicals, and electrical patterns that follow laws as precise as gravity. When Old spiritual texts, *"Be transformed by the renewing of your mind,"* it is not poetic suggestion. It is scientific instruction.

The Brain's Architecture of Faith

At birth, the human brain is a network of potential. Billions of neurons wait to be organized by experience, repetition, and attention. Over time, the thoughts you think most often become highways in this network automatic routes that determine how you interpret and react to life.

This is **neuroplasticity** — the brain's ability to rewire itself through repeated focus. Every belief you reinforce, whether empowering or destructive, becomes a physical structure. You don't just *think* a belief; you *build* it.

When you say, "I can't do this," your neurons strengthen that pathway. The next time you face a challenge, the signal travels faster, confirming the same conclusion. But when you replace that thought with "I can learn to do this," the brain begins constructing a new path — at first fragile, but growing stronger each time it's chosen.

This is why faith requires endurance. It's not that God delays the blessing; it's that your neural architecture must mature enough to carry it. Manifestation is not instant because identity must be built neuron by neuron, belief by belief.

The Reticular Activating System: The Gatekeeper of Perception

Deep within your brainstem lies a bundle of neurons called the **Reticular Activating System** (RAS). Its job is simple yet profound: to decide what you notice in reality.

You are bombarded with millions of sensory inputs every second — sounds, colors, faces, words. The RAS filters 99% of them out, showing your conscious mind only what it believes is relevant to your survival or goals.

If you constantly repeat, "Life is unfair," your RAS will faithfully highlight every unfair event and dismiss anything that contradicts it. If you say, "Opportunities are everywhere," your RAS will tune your attention to people, ideas, and openings that align with that expectation.

The RAS is neutral. It doesn't judge truth; it obeys belief. It is the biological servant of your faith.

When Jesus said, *"According to your faith be it unto you,"* He described a law that neuroscience now confirms. What you believe determines what you perceive. What you perceive shapes what you pursue. And what you pursue becomes your reality.

Faith is not wishful thinking it is selective perception. It programs your awareness to find evidence of what you hold to be true.

Dopamine: The Chemistry of Expectation

Every belief carries emotion, and emotion is chemical. The neurotransmitter **dopamine** is central to this system not merely the molecule of pleasure, but the molecule of *anticipation*.

Dopamine is released when you expect a reward, not only when you receive it. This means your mindset determines the chemical atmosphere of your brain. When you live with faith, your brain stays in a state of hopeful anticipation, which fuels motivation and resilience. You start taking consistent action because your nervous system expects a meaningful outcome.

But when belief turns cynical or fearful, dopamine production declines. The brain interprets the future as pointless, and energy disappears. You don't lose potential; you lose neurological incentive.

Faith reshapes the reward system toward endurance. It trains the brain to see progress not as instant gratification but as purpose unfolding over time. This is why disciplined believers often achieve what impulsive dreamers cannot: their chemistry is built for persistence, not thrill.

In this way, belief becomes biology's navigation system. Your thoughts determine which chemical cascades dominate your internal world dopamine for hope, serotonin for peace, cortisol for fear. The story you tell yourself becomes the environment your cells live in

Cortisol: The Silent Saboteur of Creation

Chronic stress is one of the greatest enemies of manifestation. When the brain perceives threat financial uncertainty, rejection, shame, or failure it releases **cortisol,** the stress hormone designed to keep you alive in danger.

Cortisol shuts down long-term vision to focus on immediate survival. It diverts blood flow from creative areas of the brain to primal reflex centers. It reduces dopamine sensitivity, dulls intuition, and disrupts sleep. In short, it locks you into the illusion that your future is collapsing, even when it isn't.

This is why anxiety and faith cannot coexist in the same moment not because one is moral and the other sinful, but because they operate through opposite neural states. Faith opens the mind to creation; fear closes it to preservation.

When the Bible says, *"Be still, and know that I am God,"* it is not poetic calmness it is neurobiological recalibration. Stillness lowers cortisol, restores balance to the prefrontal cortex, and reactivates higher reasoning. Peace is not passive; it's power regained.

You cannot manifest from a body locked in panic. You must first return your nervous system to safety through prayer, gratitude, order, and rest so that faith can reengage the creative circuits designed to build what you believe.

The Heart as the Subconscious Identity

In Scripture, the word *heart* appears over 800 times. But in ancient Hebrew thought, the heart was not merely emotion — it was the center of intellect, identity, and will. It represented what modern science calls the **subconscious mind** — the programming that directs behavior without conscious effort.

When Proverbs says, *"As a man thinks in his heart, so is he,"* it describes how identity, once embedded in the subconscious, overrides conscious intention. You may declare abundance, but if your heart believes lack, your actions will quietly align with limitation.

This "heart" is formed by repetition and experience. Childhood conditioning, trauma, words spoken by authority figures — all become subconscious codes. They run silently, shaping habits, relationships, and even physical health.

Renewing the mind, therefore, means reprogramming the heart. It is not memorizing new affirmations; it is reconditioning the body's emotional memory to trust in truth rather than fear. This is why transformation takes time — because neurons must relearn what safety and faith feel like.

In modern neuroscience, this process is called **emotional reconsolidation** replacing old neural patterns with new ones through repeated experience. In faith, it is called sanctification the gradual rewiring of the soul toward divine alignment. Both describe the same miracle: the rewriting of identity.

The Unity of Divine and Biological Law

The deeper you study the human system, the clearer it becomes that divine law and biological law are reflections of one design. God did not create two conflicting systems one spiritual and one scientific. He created one coherent order in which spiritual truth governs the same mechanisms that science observes.

When Old spiritual texts, *"Do not conform to this world, but be transformed by the renewing of your mind,"* it implies that the mind's renewal is the key to transformation not external events. Neuroscience agrees: change your neural pathways, and your perception of the world changes with it.

Faith, then, is not superstition. It is conscious participation in divine neuroplasticity. You are shaping the architecture of your reality by shaping the architecture of your brain.

Every prayer, every meditation, every act of forgiveness and gratitude they are not symbolic gestures; they are neurological commands that sculpt your future physiology. You are literally designing the instrument through which God plays His melody in your life.

The Invisible Machinery of Miracles

When you believe deeply, your nervous system begins to cooperate with that belief. Your muscles relax, your breathing slows, your perception widens. You notice different people, make different choices, and respond to situations with new emotional intelligence. These micro-shifts accumulate until what was once unseen becomes visible.

Miracles are not violations of natural law; they are activations of higher law laws that integrate biology, psychology, and spirit. When faith is embodied, creation becomes inevitable.

The body is not your prison; it is your amplifier. God designed it as the vessel through which invisible faith becomes tangible form. Every cell is listening to your thoughts. Every heartbeat echoes your conviction.

You do not manifest by commanding the universe; you manifest by aligning the universe within you. When mind, heart, and body harmonize in faith, reality bends to coherence.

The Quiet Revelation

Belief is not imagination. It is instruction. Your brain listens. Your cells respond. Your world reshapes around the signals you send through faith and focus.

To believe is to build. To doubt is to dismantle. The choice happens not in the heavens, but in the synapses.

When you pray, visualize, or speak truth, understand this: you are not whispering to the air. You are giving your biology a blueprint. You are teaching your nervous system how to live in alignment with divine order.

Every renewed thought becomes a seed. Every consistent belief becomes structure. Every act of faith becomes circuitry.

And as those circuits strengthen, the line between spiritual and physical dissolves revealing that they were never separate at all.

You are the bridge between both worlds. Your faith is the language your biology understands.

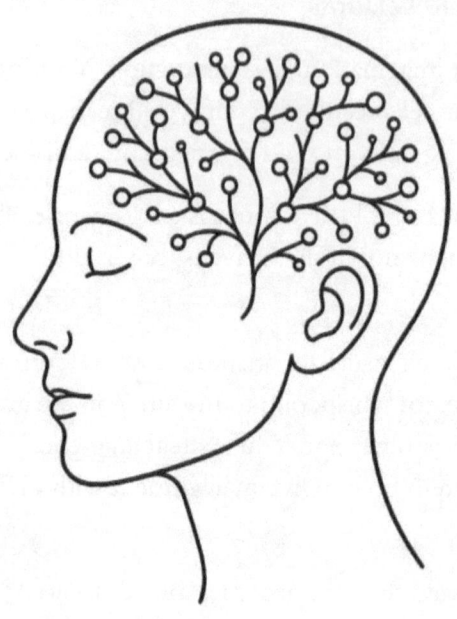

Chapter 5 – The Frequency of Thought: How the Brain Emits Reality

by Aria Vale

Everything in creation vibrates. From the hum of subatomic particles to the rotation of galaxies, existence is a spectrum of frequency. Thought is no exception. What we call "thinking" is not silent every neuron in the brain communicates through oscillations of electrical potential. These waves form rhythmic patterns that can be measured, recorded, and most importantly shaped.

For centuries, spiritual traditions claimed that thought emits energy influencing matter. Science now confirms the biological foundation of that idea. The brain is not just a storage organ; it is a transmitter and receiver, broadcasting electromagnetic fields that interact with both the body and the environment. When Jesus said, *"Let this mind be in you, which was also in Christ Jesus,"* He pointed to a state of mental coherence a frequency of unity between spirit, brain, and heart that aligns human consciousness with divine order.

The Electric Language of the Mind

Every thought begins as an electrochemical signal. Neurons fire across synapses, releasing charged ions that create microcurrents measurable as brainwaves. Using electroencephalography (EEG), scientists have mapped these rhythms into categories based on frequency: beta, alpha, theta, delta, and gamma.

Each frequency corresponds to a different state of consciousness:

- **Beta (13–30 Hz):** The waking, analytical state. High beta indicates focus and alertness, but excessive beta often driven by stress creates mental noise, anxiety, and fragmentation. Most modern people live here, caught in cognitive overdrive, unable to perceive subtle guidance or intuition.

- **Alpha (8–12 Hz):** The relaxed, creative state. Alpha waves bridge conscious and subconscious awareness, allowing ideas and intuition to flow. When people pray, daydream, or meditate, alpha activity rises. In this state, perception widens, and the nervous system enters harmony rather than defense.

- **Theta (4–7 Hz):** The deep meditative or contemplative state. Theta opens the gateway between imagination and embodiment, where the subconscious integrates new beliefs. Children under seven naturally operate in theta, which is why early experiences form identity so powerfully.

- **Gamma (30–100 Hz):** The state of peak integration. Harvard researchers in 2016 recorded unusually high gamma coherence in long-term meditators during states of compassion and focus. Gamma links distant neural regions into simultaneous harmony a biological signature of transcendence.

These waves are not random; they form a symphony of perception. The brain's frequency determines what the mind can perceive. When your neural rhythm is chaotic, your perception narrows to survival. When it is coherent, you see patterns, opportunities, and possibilities invisible to the anxious mind.

Manifestation, in its truest form, begins when the frequency of thought harmonizes with the frequency of peace.

Coherence: The Hidden Law of Order

In physics, coherence describes when separate waves synchronize into a single, organized pattern. In neuroscience, it refers to the alignment of brain regions communicating fluidly, producing clarity and insight. Spiritually, coherence is alignment with divine rhythm the moment human will ceases to fight the current of creation and begins to flow with it.

The more coherent the brain becomes, the more efficiently it processes information, generates intuition, and maintains focus. Functional MRI studies show that during prayer, gratitude, or meditative worship, the brain's prefrontal cortex (responsible for moral reasoning and foresight) synchronizes with deeper emotional centers. The result is a unified system intellect and emotion vibrating in agreement.

Dr. Andrew Newberg, a pioneer of neurotheology, observed this phenomenon in monks and nuns engaged in deep prayer. Their parietal lobes the region defining the sense of "self" grew quieter, while their frontal lobes, which regulate compassion and decision-making, became highly active. The data suggest that surrender and faith literally reshape neural activity into patterns of order and connection.

Coherence is not mystical energy; it is measurable physiology. But it also mirrors divine principle. The universe itself operates on coherence gravitational systems, harmonic ratios, atomic structure. Manifestation follows the same law: what is coherent grows stronger; what is divided collapses.

The Heart-Brain Connection

Modern science once treated the heart as nothing more than a pump. That view collapsed when neurocardiology discovered that the heart contains over **40,000 sensory neurons** capable of processing information independently of the brain. These neurons form a complex nervous network that communicates with the brain through electromagnetic and biochemical signals.

The heart generates an electromagnetic field that extends several feet beyond the body, measurable with magnetometers. This field is not static it changes with emotion. Coherent emotions like gratitude, love, and faith produce smooth, rhythmic patterns. Fear, anger, and anxiety create chaotic, irregular waves.

The HeartMath Institute's studies have shown that when people intentionally cultivate gratitude or compassion, heart rhythms become highly ordered. This "heart coherence" then entrains the brain into similar order, improving cognition, focus, and emotional regulation. The state of prayer when genuine and heartfelt creates biological harmony between the two organs that define human consciousness: heart and brain.

In this sense, manifestation is not about "sending energy" into the universe. It is about generating internal coherence so that your biological field vibrates in agreement with divine intelligence. The heart becomes the conductor, and the brain follows its rhythm.

Scripture's wisdom anticipated this centuries ago: *"Above all else, guard your heart, for everything you do flows from it."* (Proverbs 4:23). Modern data now reveal how literal that statement is. When the heart's field is chaotic, the brain's decision-making circuits degrade. When the heart is calm, the mind perceives clearly. Faith begins in the heart because coherence begins there.

Consciousness and Probability

Skeptics often argue that thought cannot influence matter. Yet decades of controlled experiments suggest otherwise. From the 1970s through the early 2000s, the **Princeton Engineering Anomalies Research (PEAR)** program tested whether focused human intention could alter random mechanical systems. Across millions of trials, small but statistically significant deviations appeared whenever human consciousness was directed toward the machines.

Later, researchers like **Dr. Dean Radin** replicated these findings with quantum-level experiments showing that observation alters probability distributions. While these effects are subtle, their implications are vast: consciousness participates in physical reality.

Manifestation, therefore, may not defy science it may reveal an incomplete understanding of it. The observer effect demonstrates that attention is not passive; it is creative. The universe is responsive, not indifferent.

If every thought is a frequency, and if matter responds to frequency, then faith sustained, coherent focus rooted in peace becomes the biological interface between the visible and invisible.

The Quantum Mirror of the Mind

Quantum physics teaches that subatomic particles exist in probability states until observed. The act of measurement collapses potential into actuality. While the human mind cannot consciously control electrons, it operates under the same principle of observation.

The Reticular Activating System, described in the previous chapter, filters reality according to belief. The quantum field operates similarly probabilities collapse around the observer's expectation. Belief, whether spiritual or scientific, is the focusing mechanism through which potential becomes form.

When Scripture says, *"Faith is the substance of things hoped for, the evidence of things not seen,"* it describes the same mechanism in spiritual language. Faith is not mere optimism; it is coherent observation sustained long enough for the invisible pattern to crystallize into physical order.

The Divine Frequency

Harvard's 2016 gamma study revealed that during advanced meditation, participants exhibited remarkable **gamma synchrony** across the brain waves oscillating at roughly 40 Hz in perfect coherence. These individuals described feelings of unity, timelessness, and boundless clarity.

From a spiritual lens, this state resembles the "mind of Christ" a consciousness so attuned to divine truth that separation dissolves. In gamma coherence, the brain no longer operates as fragmented regions but as one integrated system. Similarly, divine alignment fuses intellect, emotion, and spirit into a single harmonic current.

This unity is what Scripture calls *peace beyond understanding*. Neurologically, it is not numbness but synchronization the nervous system vibrating at frequencies of order, love, and awareness that transcend ordinary perception.

When a person lives in this state, their thoughts carry resonance. Speech becomes precise. Intention becomes directive. Their electromagnetic field radiates coherence that subtly influences environments and people. It is not manipulation it is magnetism born from order.

The Field of Faith

Every biological process emits electromagnetic patterns. The heart, brain, and even DNA communicate through light and frequency. Physicists refer to the fabric connecting all particles as the quantum field; Scripture calls it the Spirit that fills all things. Different language, same law.

When you think, pray, or believe, you modulate this field through bioelectrical coherence. The stronger the harmony between your mind, heart, and nervous system, the clearer the signal. Prayer is not broadcasting requests into the sky; it is tuning your entire being into divine resonance so that reality echoes the same order.

Faith, then, is measurable coherence an alignment of thought, emotion, and physiology so precise that probability reorganizes around it.

The Human Transmitter

Your body is not a container for faith; it is the instrument through which faith becomes physical.

The brain emits, the heart modulates, and the spirit directs. Together they form a triad electromagnetic, biochemical, and divine.

When your mind races in fear, the signal becomes static. When your heart steadies in trust, coherence returns. And when both vibrate in the same frequency of peace, reality begins to mirror that harmony.

True manifestation is not "energy magic." It is bio-electrical agreement with divine law. The mind becomes ordered, the heart synchronized, and the body grounded in trust. In that state, creation responds not out of manipulation, but recognition as if the universe itself says, *"This one is speaking in My frequency."*

The human being is a living transmitter of faith. Every heartbeat and every neural pulse declares a frequency that shapes experience. The moment thought and emotion merge in coherence, heaven and earth touch.

The mystery was never distant or esoteric. It was biological. It was built into your design.

When your brain and heart vibrate as one when faith becomes physiology manifestation ceases to be an act of will and becomes the natural language of life itself

The Frequency of Thought:
How the Brain Emits Reality

by Aria Vale

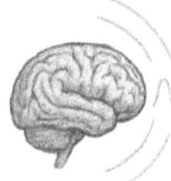

Coherence:
The hidden
law of order

BETA (13-30 Hz)
ALPHA (8-12 Hz)
THETA (4-7 Hz)
DELTA (0.5-3 Hz)
GAMMA (30-100 Hz)

Manifestation begins
when thonght harmonizes
with pesce

Coherence:
The hidden law
of order

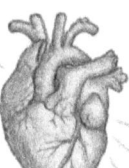

Chapter 6 – The Architecture of Time: Why Manifestation Requires Delay

by Aria Vale

Human beings experience time as movement a sequence of moments unfolding one after another. Yet to the mind of God, all possibilities already exist. Time is not a barrier between you and what you seek; it is the bridge that makes manifestation sustainable. Without time, growth could not occur, identity could not stabilize, and faith would have no meaning.

The illusion of delay frustrates those who misunderstand its purpose. They pray, visualize, and act, but when results do not appear instantly, they assume something has gone wrong. In truth, the waiting period is not punishment; it is integration. Time is the nervous system of creation, weaving potential into pattern.

Time as the Nervous System of Reality

Modern physics describes time not as a separate force but as a dimension interwoven with space. Every event occurs within this continuum, giving reality order and sequence. Spiritually, the same structure governs manifestation: divine timing is not random it's mathematical. It regulates the maturation of both the manifestation and the manifester.

If you received everything you desired instantly, you would collapse under the weight of unintegrated change. The nervous system, the psyche, and even the identity must adapt to new conditions before they can sustain them. Time is the mechanism that allows this adaptation.

A seed planted in the soil does not resist its darkness; it uses it. The pressure and heat that seem to delay growth are precisely what activate it. The same principle governs your desires: every delay is germination.

The Brain's Perception of Time

The human brain does not measure time mechanically; it constructs it biologically. Research in neuroscience shows that **theta-gamma synchronization** a rhythmic interaction between two brainwave frequencies plays a central role in how we perceive the passage of moments. Theta waves (slow, cyclical) provide the framework of continuity, while gamma bursts (rapid and precise) fill those intervals with sensory detail.

Together, they allow the brain to experience flow rather than chaos. If either rhythm becomes disrupted through stress, impatience, or overstimulation our sense of time fractures. Minutes feel like hours, or weeks vanish in distraction.

This neurological rhythm mirrors spiritual timing. Faith maintains theta's steady rhythm patience, expectation, calm while inspired action mirrors gamma's precision. The balance between them creates coherence, the inner state where manifestation aligns naturally with divine order. Impatience breaks that rhythm, scattering the mind's focus and delaying the very outcome it seeks.

The Prefrontal Cortex and Temporal Foresight

The prefrontal cortex, the brain's executive center, is responsible for long-term vision and decision-making. It allows humans to imagine the future, delay gratification, and plan actions that serve goals beyond immediate reward.

Psychological research on **delayed gratification**, beginning with the famous Stanford marshmallow experiment, revealed a crucial truth: those who could wait for a greater future reward consistently achieved more stability, success, and emotional health throughout life. Neuroscientists later discovered why these individuals displayed stronger communication between the prefrontal cortex and the limbic system, meaning their higher reasoning could regulate emotional impulses.

Spiritually, this is the architecture of faith. Waiting is not passivity; it is neurological mastery. The mind that can delay gratification for the sake of purpose is biologically aligned with the divine principle of timing. In contrast, impulsive impatience floods the brain with cortisol, narrowing perception and severing connection to long-term vision.

Manifestation, therefore, is not only spiritual maturity it is cognitive maturity. God entrusts fulfillment to minds capable of sustaining it.

The Dopamine Curve of Anticipation

The neurotransmitter **dopamine** often mislabeled the "pleasure chemical" is actually the messenger of anticipation. It rises not when we receive a reward, but when we expect one. This design ensures motivation, curiosity, and movement toward the unseen.

When faith is steady, dopamine maintains healthy cycles of anticipation, keeping the brain engaged and resilient. But when impatience takes over when one demands the outcome now the system collapses. The dopamine curve crashes, leading to discouragement, anxiety, and loss of motivation.

God's timing is structured to train this system. He stretches anticipation to build endurance. When Old spiritual texts, *"To everything there is a season, and a time for every purpose under heaven,"* it describes this neurochemical truth. Seasons protect you from spiritual overstimulation they regulate the rhythm of desire and fulfillment so that gratitude, not greed, becomes your baseline.

Identity Integration Through Waiting

Psychology teaches that the self is not a static entity; it is a process of integration. Each new experience must be woven into the narrative of identity before it feels natural. Without time, the psyche would fragment under sudden change.

This explains why manifestation often pauses at the threshold of fulfillment. The external opportunity may already exist, but the internal structure required to hold it has not yet formed. Waiting allows your subconscious identity the "heart" described in Scripture to realign with your conscious intention.

If success or love arrives before your nervous system and beliefs have adjusted, self-sabotage follows. The mind will unconsciously reject what it cannot stabilize. Divine delay prevents collapse. It gives you space to become compatible with your own prayer.

In neuroscience, this process resembles **memory reconsolidation** when the brain rewrites old emotional patterns to accommodate new truth. Spiritually, it is sanctification: becoming prepared for the weight of answered prayer.

Quantum Stability and Observer Maturity

At the subatomic level, particles exist as probabilities until observed, a phenomenon known as **quantum superposition.** When observation occurs, the wave collapses into one outcome a process physicists call **decoherence.**

For coherence to stabilize, the observer must remain consistent; fluctuating attention produces unstable patterns. This parallels human manifestation: your focus collapses possibility into reality only when it remains steady long enough for probability to organize.

In quantum mechanics, time acts as the stabilizing dimension that allows this collapse to occur coherently. Without time, energy would exist in pure potential, never forming structure. Likewise, divine timing ensures that your faith remains coherent sustained, not sporadic so the manifestation can crystallize without distortion.

The "waiting" you experience is often the system ensuring observer stability. God withholds premature arrival not to deny you, but to prevent incoherence.

The Spiritual Geometry of Seasons

Divine timing operates like geometry precise, relational, and ordered. The Book of Ecclesiastes states, *"To everything there is a season."* Each phase of waiting, working, and receiving is a line segment in the architecture of purpose.

When you resist this structure, impatience bends the geometry. You begin to rush processes that require gestation. You dig up seeds to check their progress, destroying the rhythm that sustains growth.

Faith, by contrast, honors sequence. It knows that every season carries its own sacred frequency. The delay between sowing and reaping is not emptiness; it is the silence where unseen roots form strength.

To live in harmony with divine timing is to trust that the Designer measures precisely when your system can bear the weight of fulfillment. What appears as distance is actually protection a calibration between desire and destiny.

Impatience as Neurological Disorder

Impatience is not merely emotional; it is physiological fragmentation. When you fixate on absence, the amygdala signals threat. Cortisol floods the bloodstream, narrowing perception and disrupting synchronization between the brain's hemispheres. The result is distorted timing your internal clock accelerates, producing restlessness and tunnel vision.

Faith reverses this. Through prayer, stillness, or gratitude, the prefrontal cortex reasserts control, reestablishing coherence between limbic emotion and higher reasoning. Time feels spacious again. The nervous system realigns with divine rhythm.

In this biological sense, patience is not waiting *longer* it is waiting *coherently*. It restores harmony between perception and process.

The Sacred Utility of Delay

Delay is the scaffolding that holds reality as it takes shape. Without duration, lessons could not imprint, virtues could not mature, and transformation would collapse into impulse. Time stretches the soul so that revelation can settle into wisdom.

Even in physics, structure arises through interval: waves need cycles, matter needs vibration, and growth needs repetition. Creation itself breathes through time. The divine uses waiting not to test your endurance but to synchronize you with eternity's tempo.

You are not being held back; you are being tuned.

A Living Metaphor

A seed placed in soil experiences three phases: burial, silence, and emergence. To the impatient observer, nothing happens for days. Yet inside the shell, molecular architecture shifts proteins unfold, energy redirects, and roots push against resistance. If the shell broke too soon, the plant would die.

Time is that darkness the sacred containment where potential reorganizes before light. Your manifestation is no different. What feels like stillness is biochemical, spiritual, and quantum reconfiguration. God's timing is the pressure that ensures form can hold spirit without fracture.

The Revelation of Time

We think of time as distance, but it is actually order. It is the divine method of translation how possibility becomes experience without chaos.

Every moment of delay shapes the consciousness that will receive the result. Each day of waiting builds neurological, emotional, and spiritual compatibility with what is to come. In this way, time is not external; it is internal growth made visible.

When impatience fades, perception changes. You no longer chase outcomes; you synchronize with them. You realize that manifestation is not about speed but symmetry the alignment of soul and sequence.

Time is God's invisible architecture, the silent geometry through which creation learns to sustain itself. It does not punish; it prepares. It does not withhold; it refines.

And when the structure is complete when your belief, biology, and purpose resonate in harmony the delay dissolves, and the manifestation appears, right on time.

The Architecture of Time
by Aria Vale

Chapter 7 – The Human Mirror: Stories of Faith in Motion

by Aria Vale

Every truth about manifestation reveals itself most clearly in people in the quiet, ordinary lives where belief meets resistance and choice meets time. Principles are not born in theory; they unfold in the human heart. The stories that follow are not tales of instant miracles, but of slow alignment, small corrections, and faith taking form through motion.

---

1. The Waiter Who Started Walking

Elias worked nights at a small café downtown. He'd once dreamed of studying architecture, but years of financial pressure had buried that ambition. Every morning on his way to work, he repeated affirmations about "becoming successful," yet each evening he went home exhausted and quietly resentful that nothing changed.

One night after closing, a coworker mentioned that an online university nearby offered low-cost evening courses in design. Elias's first reaction was defensive: *I don't have the time, the money, or the focus for that anymore.* But the thought wouldn't leave.

A week later, instead of repeating his usual affirmations, he filled out the enrollment form. It was a small, trembling action but it broke years of passivity.

Months passed. He studied on buses, saved tips, and fell asleep over blueprints. Two years later, when an architectural firm opened a trainee position, Elias applied not because he felt ready, but because his habits had made him capable.

When he told me his story, he said, "I used to think manifestation was waiting for signs. Now I see the sign was the step itself."

That was the law of **aligned action** at work faith expressed through motion. The universe didn't move until he did.

---

2. The Mother Who Counted Pennies

Lydia was a single mother of two, working part-time at a grocery store. She prayed constantly for financial breakthrough. "I just want God to bless me," she told me once, tears filling her eyes. "But it feels like He's not listening."

When I asked how she managed her money, she laughed. "Manage? I just survive."

I suggested she write down every expense for one month nothing more. She resisted, embarrassed by the simplicity of it. But she did it. And when the month ended, she saw patterns she'd never noticed small leaks that added up to days of freedom she didn't know she could afford.

That single act of attention birthed transformation. She created a simple budget, saved a few dollars weekly, and began paying debts methodically. Within a year, she started selling handmade soaps at the local market. It wasn't wealth yet, but it was movement and peace.

Lydia learned **stewardship**, the forgotten law that multiplies what is honored. "I kept asking for more," she said, "but God wanted to see if I could care for little."

Her story reminded me that abundance is rarely a windfall; it's the reward of order. Divine law never gives increase to chaos.

3. The Engineer and the Empty Season

Darius was a mechanical engineer who had lost his job during a corporate downsizing. Logical, disciplined, and proud of his efficiency, he couldn't tolerate the uncertainty of unemployment. He spent six months sending resumes, each rejection tightening the coil of frustration.

When we spoke, he said bitterly, "I'm doing everything right, but it feels like nothing's moving."

I asked him a question that startled him: "What if the delay is not punishment, but calibration?"

He resisted the idea. But as weeks turned into months, something shifted. He began volunteering at a local technical school, teaching young students basic robotics. "It gave my days structure," he told me later. "I stopped counting what I'd lost and started giving what I still had."

Three months after that, one of the parents he'd taught offered him a contract role one that eventually evolved into a permanent position leading a research team.

Darius's season of silence had not been empty. It had been alignment in disguise. Through service, he reconnected his skill with purpose. The **architecture of time** had done its quiet work.

He later said, "I see now that God wasn't delaying the result He was repairing the receiver."

---

4. The Teacher Who Prayed for Peace

Amara, a high school teacher, came to me after suffering from chronic anxiety. She practiced visualization, journaling, and positive affirmations, but nothing touched the underlying tension. "I'm supposed to be grateful," she said, "but I'm always on edge."

During a session of guided prayer, we focused on her heartbeat slow, rhythmic, grounding. I asked her to breathe until she could feel its pulse without effort. As her body calmed, her mind followed. That was the first time she experienced **coherence** the alignment between thought and physiology.

In the weeks that followed, Amara made a small ritual: before entering the classroom, she would place her hand over her chest and whisper, *Peace begins here*.

Her students noticed the change first. The classroom became calmer, her voice steadier. "It's like my body learned faith before my mind did," she told me later.

She discovered that manifestation isn't just mental it's biological. When the body and spirit agree, the external world responds.

Amara's journey was proof that divine order doesn't require control. It requires resonance.

---

5. The Young Couple and the Long Road

Mira and Jonas were newly married, full of hope, and equally full of tension. They had prayed for a home, but every attempt to buy or rent ended in disappointment. "We must be doing something wrong," Jonas said. "We tithe, we plan, we pray but doors keep closing."

When I met them, I asked, "What if those doors are closing to teach rhythm, not rejection?"

Months passed. Instead of rushing, they began simplifying. They sold unnecessary things, reduced debt, and started visiting neighborhoods on weekends not to search, but to learn. They met people, listened to stories, and redefined what "home" meant.

Almost a year later, a friend introduced them to an elderly couple looking for caretakers of a small property outside town a house they could live in while paying minimal rent. It wasn't what they had envisioned, but it was peace. Over time, they renovated it, turning it into a shared community garden.

Mira said, "It wasn't the house we prayed for. It was the life we didn't know we needed."

Their story revealed how **faith and delay** often walk together how divine timing builds identity before it grants possession.

6. The Janitor and the Light

Samuel worked as a janitor in a hospital. His hours were long, his pay modest. He had every reason to feel invisible. Yet every night, he hummed softly as he mopped the corridors. When I asked once what kept him so calm, he said, "I clean as if God Himself will walk here tomorrow."

He never read a self-help book, never attended a seminar, yet he lived the purest form of manifestation: presence through purpose. His quiet faith gave him dignity in the smallest task.

Months later, the hospital director noticed his consistency and offered him a maintenance supervisor role. "It's strange," he said to me afterward. "I wasn't trying to attract anything. I was just being faithful."

Samuel's story is the human face of **stewardship and alignment** the natural law that reward follows integrity, not strategy.

---

7. The Artist Who Let Go

Nina, a painter, spent years trying to gain recognition. She submitted work to galleries, hustled commissions, and lived in constant self-doubt. One evening, she told me, "I'm exhausted from believing in something that doesn't believe in me."

I told her, "Maybe your faith isn't exhausted it's evolving. Stop chasing the outcome. Paint for God, not for proof."

For three months she stopped promoting and simply painted whatever she felt during prayer: clouds, hands, eyes, silence. She posted nothing online, shared nothing publicly.

When she finally returned to her studio's open exhibition, a visiting curator stopped before one of her new pieces a quiet painting titled *Stillness Between Miracles*. He offered her a commission the following week.

Nina didn't manifest success; she mirrored surrender. When faith ceases to demand, it begins to receive.

Reflections

Each of these lives shows the same divine mechanics from different angles. The laws are constant; the stories are human.

Elias found that faith requires motion.
Lydia learned that responsibility multiplies.
Darius discovered that waiting integrates.
Amara felt coherence turn fear into peace.
Mira and Jonas realized timing matures identity.
Samuel embodied purpose in the ordinary.
Nina revealed the beauty of surrender.

Every manifestation is a mirror reflecting the state of the soul that creates it. The universe does not respond to desire alone; it reflects structure, stewardship, coherence, and trust.

We often imagine faith as reaching upward, but it is also looking inward. The divine speaks through daily acts the form signed, the debt paid, the kindness given, the silence accepted.

When I look at these stories, I see one truth repeated in infinite forms: manifestation is not a moment of magic, but a movement of faith made visible through time. Each act of trust ripples through creation until reality, like a mirror, returns the image refined and whole.

And in that reflection, we see ourselves not as beggars of blessings, but as participants in a divine architecture living proof that the laws of manifestation are not abstract forces, but the rhythm of God breathing through human motion.

Chapter 8 – The Law of Resistance: Why Opposition Is Proof of Alignment

by Aria Vale

Every movement toward transformation produces tension. It is not a flaw in the system it *is* the system. Resistance is not evidence that something has gone wrong; it is confirmation that something has started moving. Like friction under acceleration, opposition arises only when energy begins to change direction.

In manifestation, the moment faith becomes action, the environment internal and external reorganizes to test stability. What you feel as struggle is reality recalibrating around your new frequency.

The Physics of Friction

In physics, motion creates resistance. The faster an object accelerates, the greater the friction opposing it. Without friction, there would be no traction; without opposition, movement would never stabilize.

Spiritual growth follows the same principle. When you begin aligning with truth acting differently, thinking higher, speaking with integrity the forces that once held you in place react. Not because you are wrong, but because momentum demands balance.

Resistance, therefore, is not an obstacle to manifestation. It is the byproduct of momentum.

The Biology of Resistance

Inside the human body, every change triggers a response called **homeostasis** the drive to maintain equilibrium. The nervous system prefers predictability; it equates familiarity with safety, even when familiar patterns cause pain.

When you start believing or behaving in new ways, the brain interprets it as threat. Cortisol levels rise. The amygdala fires alarms. Old neural pathways, wired by years of repetition, fight to stay alive.

This is why the first steps of transformation often feel worse than before. The system is not sabotaging you it is protecting what it knows.

Neuroscientists call this the **comfort zone effect.** When you introduce new patterns whether exercising, setting boundaries, or pursuing a goal the prefrontal cortex and limbic system clash. Logic says "go forward," but the emotional brain says "this is unsafe."

Until repetition rewires these circuits, your body will resist. This is biological resistance proof that change is real.

Hormesis: Growth Through Stress

In biology, the term **hormesis** describes how small doses of stress strengthen an organism. Exercise, fasting, cold exposure, even learning each introduces temporary strain that triggers adaptation.

Muscles tear before they grow. The immune system strengthens by facing microbes. The mind expands through confusion before comprehension.

Spiritual manifestation works through the same law. Every challenge that appears when you act in faith is a controlled stressor training the soul for capacity.

People often pray for expansion but reject the pressure that expansion requires. They ask for strength but avoid resistance. Yet the very friction they resist is what makes their faith functional.

The Ego's Last Defense

Psychological resistance often disguises itself as logic. Doubt, procrastination, or fatigue surface precisely when progress is near. These are not random they are defense mechanisms of the **ego**, the self-image built on past identity.

The ego's job is stability. It keeps you consistent with who you *believe* you are. So when you start thinking, acting, or speaking as a higher version of yourself, the ego panics. It whispers rational excuses: *Maybe I should wait. Maybe this isn't the right time.*

But that discomfort is the shedding of identity. You are not regressing you are outgrowing.

In neuroscience, this moment is known as a **prediction error.** The brain's dopamine system forecasts rewards based on familiar behavior. When you act differently beyond its prediction the expected reward doesn't arrive, and dopamine dips. This temporary "low" feels like doubt or disappointment. But it is actually the moment your brain learns something new.

Spiritual evolution depends on this cycle: expectation → disruption → integration. The discomfort is the rewiring process itself.

The Two Interpretations of Resistance

There are only two ways to interpret resistance. The first says, *This is a sign I should stop.* The second says, *This is a sign I'm crossing the threshold.*

The first keeps you enslaved to comfort; the second transforms you.

When people experience sudden chaos after acting on faith finances tightening, relationships shifting, emotions surfacing they often assume the universe is rejecting them. But the opposite is true. Energy is rearranging. Hidden dependencies are being exposed. False alignments are dissolving.

You prayed for growth; now the pruning begins.

Resistance is not punishment it is preparation.

Iron and Fire

"Iron sharpens iron." The process produces sparks, sound, and heat but the edge emerges only through friction.

Jesus faced wilderness before ministry. Moses faced the desert before deliverance. Every calling introduces confrontation, because higher identity cannot coexist with old conditions.

Even nature mirrors this law: a seed must split before growth. Pressure from soil and gravity triggers the enzymes that awaken life. What looks like destruction is activation.

In manifestation, resistance is the heat that hardens faith into structure. Without it, belief remains theory.

Story 1: The Freelancer and the Storm

Janelle left her corporate job to start her design business. She prayed for guidance, made a plan, and took the leap. Within weeks, clients canceled, her laptop broke, and her savings dwindled.

She panicked. "Did I misread the signs?" she asked.

But instead of retreating, she stayed the course. She adapted borrowed equipment, learned new software, and worked through sleepless nights.

Months later, the clients who had left returned, now referring others. "Looking back," she said, "that chaos wasn't rejection. It burned away everything weak in me."

Her resistance was confirmation faith in motion. The energy she had released needed friction to stabilize.

Story 2: The Silence Before the Song

Ethan, a musician, had always written songs for others but dreamed of performing his own. The night he decided to book his first show, his voice failed during rehearsal. A week later, he got sick, his car broke down, and fear whispered that it was a sign to quit.

But deep down he knew it was the same pattern that had stopped him before the ego protecting old identity. He rested, recovered, and played anyway. The performance was small, imperfect, but alive.

Later, he realized that his voice hadn't failed; it had *reset*. The strain had strengthened it.

Resistance had refined resonance literally and spiritually.

The Nervous System and Faith

When pressure rises, the sympathetic nervous system triggers fight, flight, or freeze. The body floods with cortisol, heart rate increases, perception narrows. Most people interpret this physiological alert as "something is wrong."

But the signal only means: *Something is changing.*

Faith is the act of reinterpreting stress. Instead of retreating, you breathe, regulate, and move through it. Over time, the parasympathetic system reclaims balance, proving to the body that growth is safe.

This process rewires emotional memory. What once triggered fear becomes integrated as strength. Every round of resistance builds tolerance, expanding the nervous system's capacity for creation.

Resistance as Calibration

Manifestation requires coherence alignment between thought, emotion, and action. Resistance exposes the parts that are not yet aligned. It is the feedback mechanism of creation.

If your desire is authentic but your belief contradicts it, resistance will surface as internal conflict. If your words say faith but your habits reflect fear, resistance will emerge externally as delay or frustration.

It's not punishment; it's calibration God's way of highlighting dissonance so harmony can emerge.

The Refining Fire

Metals are purified through heat. Impurities surface only when temperature rises. Likewise, pressure in life reveals what must be released.

Resistance refines belief from fantasy into faith. Fantasy avoids difficulty; faith endures it.

When opposition appears, you are not being tested for worth you are being tempered for capacity. The delay, the tension, the fear they are fire shaping form.

The prophet Isaiah wrote, *"I have refined you, but not as silver; I have tested you in the furnace of affliction."* Manifestation is that furnace burning away disbelief until only coherence remains.

The Moment Before Breakthrough

Psychologically, breakthroughs often follow collapse. Studies on behavioral change show that the brain experiences a final spike in stress before adaptation occurs a threshold effect. The nervous system resists until it can no longer sustain the old pattern, then suddenly reorganizes.

This moment feels like failure. It is, in fact, the final contraction before birth.

People give up here because pain convinces them they've gone too far. But from the divine view, this is the evidence that manifestation has begun the new identity forming beneath the friction.

The Revelation

Resistance is not rejection; it is refinement. Every surge of fear, every closed door, every unexpected obstacle is confirmation that your energy is real enough to be measured. Only movement creates opposition.

When pressure appears, the universe is not saying *no* it is stretching to accommodate the new version of you. The nervous system adjusts, the environment reshapes, and identity evolves.

The seed breaks. The fire burns. The iron sharpens.

That is not destruction. That is creation responding.

Resistance is divine feedback the sound of transformation under construction. And when you learn to interpret it not as threat but as proof of motion, you will realize that friction is the language of growth.

Manifestation has already begun the moment you feel the weight pushing back.

Chapter 9 – The Law of Rest: The Silence After Alignment

by Aria Vale

Creation begins with movement but completes in stillness. Every pulse of life follows this rhythm expansion and rest, inhale and exhale, labor and Sabbath. Yet most people try to manifest through endless motion, mistaking exhaustion for devotion. They forget that the universe itself breathes, and that after alignment comes stillness the sacred silence where manifestation settles into form.

True creation is not the noise of doing but the quiet of becoming. Rest is not retreat; it is integration.

The Physiology of Completion

Every living system depends on cycles of effort and recovery. In the body, the growth we associate with strength, learning, and vitality happens not during activity but during restoration.

When you exercise, muscles tear microscopically. The rebuilding occurs afterward through rest, nutrition, and sleep. During deep sleep stages, growth hormone surges, tissues regenerate, and the immune system resets. Similarly, the brain consolidates memory and learning during REM cycles.

In neuroscience, this process is called **neural consolidation** the translation of temporary electrical patterns into lasting structures. Each new insight, habit, or skill you acquire is fragile until it passes through rest. The quiet hours between effort are when neural circuits stabilize and knowledge becomes identity.

Manifestation follows the same law. You labor in faith, take aligned action, endure resistance and then you must let go. The nervous system needs space to integrate the new pattern of belief and behavior. Without rest, the new identity cannot solidify; it remains conceptual, unembodied.

This is why breakthroughs often come after surrender. The body catches up to what the spirit already knows.

The Parasympathetic Key

Biologically, rest is governed by the **parasympathetic nervous system** the "rest and digest" counterpart to the adrenaline-fueled fight-or-flight response. When this system activates, heart rate slows, muscles relax, digestion improves, and the mind shifts from vigilance to repair.

Modern neuroscience has identified another critical player: the **default-mode network (DMN)** a set of brain regions that activates during quiet reflection, daydreaming, or prayerful stillness. This network integrates information, connects seemingly unrelated ideas, and restores emotional balance.

The DMN is where creativity hides. When you stop forcing solutions, the brain's associative pathways open. Insights surface uninvited like light filtering through still water.

Every artist, engineer, and scientist who has experienced a "eureka moment" has unknowingly accessed this biological Sabbath. The conscious mind stops pushing, and the subconscious finally speaks.

In spiritual language, this is the whisper after the storm: *"Be still and know."*

The Psychological Resistance to Stillness

Many people cannot rest even when they have earned it. They achieve, succeed, or manifest something and then feel an unexpected emptiness. Psychologists call this **post-achievement depression** the crash that follows completion.

It occurs because the brain, conditioned by constant stimulation, loses its external goal and panics in the absence of motion. Dopamine, the neurotransmitter of anticipation, drops sharply once a target is reached.

The result is restlessness, irritability, even guilt for pausing.

Spiritually, this is the ego's resistance to silence. It equates being with doing, value with productivity. Yet without rest, the system overheats; progress becomes noise without integration.

The Law of Rest reminds us that manifestation matures through surrender. Stillness is not laziness it is the nervous system returning to coherence after faith's exertion.

Sabbath: The Science of Trust

The ancient Sabbath principle was not a religious restriction but a biological revelation. God Himself modeled it: six days of creation followed by a day of rest not because He was weary, but because completion required pause.

When Old spiritual texts, *"God blessed the seventh day and sanctified it,"* it implies that rest itself carries creative power. The blessing was not in the work but in the stillness that sealed it.

Even the land obeys this rhythm. Ancient farmers allowed soil to lie fallow every seventh year, letting minerals and microorganisms replenish. Continuous planting depletes fertility; rest restores it.

Likewise, your inner soil mind, body, and spirit needs intervals of silence to regenerate. The pause is not wasted time; it is invisible cultivation.

Jesus in the Storm

One of the most paradoxical moments in the Gospels is when Jesus sleeps through a violent storm while His disciples panic. When they wake Him, terrified, He calms the sea with a word.

That story is not about supernatural control it is about coherence. While chaos raged outside, His internal state remained undisturbed. Rest in that moment was not inactivity; it was authority.

The storm represents life's volatility. The sleep represents faith's physiology an aligned nervous system so grounded in divine trust that fear loses its signal.

The Law of Rest teaches that peace is not what happens after the storm passes. It is the consciousness that silences the storm.

The Writer Who Forgot to Breathe

Sofia was a novelist whose third book had stalled for months. She wrote late into the night, consumed by deadlines, rewriting paragraphs until dawn. The more she pushed, the less inspired she felt. "I thought I was losing my gift," she told me.

When I asked when she last took a break, she laughed nervously. "I can't afford to stop. I'll fall behind."

I asked her to stop anyway for one week. No writing, no editing, no screens. She resisted but agreed.

The first two days, she was restless. By the fourth, something softened. She walked without headphones, sat under trees, and read poetry aloud to no one.

On the seventh day, an idea arrived effortlessly the missing thread connecting her entire story. She described it as if it had "found her."

In truth, it had always been there, waiting beneath the noise.

Stillness did not cost her progress; it returned her rhythm. Rest reopened the neural channels that creativity required.

The Business Owner Who Let Go

Evan ran a small design firm that had grown rapidly. After two years of nonstop work, he felt trapped in success exhausted, irritable, unable to think clearly. "I built what I wanted," he said, "but I'm too drained to enjoy it."

He decided to take a month-long sabbatical, something he had avoided out of fear that everything would collapse. In the first week, he barely slept his mind raced with unfinished tasks. But gradually, something changed. His breathing slowed. He noticed birdsong in the morning for the first time in years.

Halfway through his rest, an unexpected realization surfaced: he'd been expanding his company faster than his purpose could sustain. The constant strain was not from work but from misalignment.

When he returned, he simplified operations, delegated more, and refocused on the kind of design that originally inspired him. Profit stabilized, but more importantly, peace returned.

Evan's rest did not weaken his business; it recalibrated it.

The Neurobiology of Peace

During deep rest sleep, meditation, or prayer the brain enters alpha and theta states, characterized by slow, harmonious electrical rhythms. In these frequencies, the prefrontal cortex quiets, the amygdala calms, and the hippocampus integrates memory.

Functional MRI studies show that during such states, the **default-mode network** strengthens its connections, particularly between the medial prefrontal cortex and posterior cingulate cortex regions linked to self-awareness and empathy.

This biological coherence mirrors spiritual peace. When internal systems synchronize, energy once spent on defense becomes available for creation. The result is clarity without effort, insight without struggle.

Rest, therefore, is not absence of productivity it is the highest form of it. The brain reorganizes, the heart rate steadies, the immune system regenerates. You become a clearer channel for divine intelligence.

Rest as Receptivity

Constant striving narrows perception. You see only obstacles and outcomes. But rest widens awareness it opens the perceptual field to include what was previously unseen.

This is why breakthroughs often arrive in moments of quiet. When you stop grasping, you become receptive. The mind no longer filters possibilities through tension; it listens.

The world's noise says, *keep pushing.* Divine order says, *pause, and let what you've built breathe.*

Rest is receptivity the feminine side of manifestation. It allows the universe to respond.

The Silence After Alignment

Rest is not a break from creation; it is its completion. Every cycle of manifestation ends in stillness because stillness is the state of trust. You cannot hold onto the seed and expect it to grow. You plant, water, and then you wait.

Faith's final expression is rest the willingness to let the process finish itself.

When you stop forcing, the nervous system shifts from defense to integration. The heart's rhythm steadies, the brain's waves harmonize, and reality begins to organize around coherence.

This is the silence after alignment the soft hum when action and surrender meet.

The Divine Seal

In every creative act, rest is the signature at the end the quiet punctuation that tells the universe the work is complete. The artist steps back from the canvas, the builder lays down the final stone, the believer exhales and releases the outcome.

In that exhale, manifestation seals.

Stillness does not mean nothing is happening; it means everything is. Invisible systems continue aligning, multiplying, and stabilizing. The harvest ripens while the soil sleeps.

Rest is God's final movement in the symphony of creation the pause that turns sound into music, effort into expression, and faith into form.

It is the divine seal on manifestation the moment heaven confirms, integrates, and multiplies what faith has built.

So when silence comes after striving, do not rush to fill it. Let it breathe through you. For in that quiet, creation completes itself.

Chapter 10 – The Law of the Hidden Order: How Chaos Conceals Precision

by Aria Vale

There is a moment in every transformation when life stops making sense. Plans dissolve, structures collapse, and the familiar becomes unrecognizable. It feels like punishment or error, yet it is the moment closest to truth. What we call chaos is not the breakdown of order it is order beyond our resolution. The divine pattern does not disappear when we lose sight of it; it simply descends beneath the threshold of comprehension.

The Law of the Hidden Order reveals that chaos is not random. It is structure unfolding in ways too intricate for the linear mind to trace. Just as galaxies spiral from turbulence, so do destinies emerge from disruption.

The Mathematics of Apparent Disorder

Modern science once believed that the universe followed clean, predictable rules until chaos theory dismantled that illusion. In the 1960s, meteorologist Edward Lorenz discovered that tiny variations in initial conditions could produce wildly different outcomes. This became known as the **butterfly effect** the idea that the flap of a butterfly's wings might influence a hurricane weeks later.

At first, this seemed to prove that nature was unstable. But deeper study revealed something astonishing: beneath the unpredictability lay exquisite patterns. When scientists plotted these complex systems weather, heart rhythms, planetary orbits they found that chaos had shape.

These shapes were called **strange attractors** hidden geometric structures that guided seemingly random behavior toward organized patterns. No two paths were identical, yet every line obeyed an unseen symmetry.

Fractals mathematical figures that repeat their structure at every scale exposed the same truth. The veins of a leaf mirror the branching of rivers, the pattern of lungs, the flow of galaxies. What looks chaotic at one level reveals precision when seen from another.

The same law governs human life. What appears as confusion, loss, or coincidence is often a fractal of divine intelligence too vast for the immediate mind to recognize.

The Divine Architecture of Chaos

Scripture captures this mystery in a single phrase: *"All things work together for good to them that love God."* Notice it does not say *all things are good*. It says they *work together* a phrase of process, not comfort. Divine order is rarely visible in real time; it unfolds through contrast, conflict, and collapse.

From a higher dimension, chaos is choreography. The storm is not error; it is recalibration. When life seems to fall apart, you are watching the blueprint rearrange itself into coherence.

Creation itself was born from apparent chaos. The Genesis narrative begins not with perfection but with formlessness: *"The earth was without form, and void; and darkness was upon the face of the deep."* Out of that void came structure, species, light. God's first act of manifestation began in the dark.

Faith, then, is not blind optimism it is trust in the unseen mathematics of grace.

The Psychology of Falling Apart

When a person's life fractures, the mind interprets it as failure. Relationships end, jobs disappear, identities crumble, and the psyche screams, *Something has gone wrong*. But psychology recognizes another process at work: **cognitive restructuring.**

The brain cannot hold two contradictory truths indefinitely. When new information collides with old identity, the existing structure must break. This disintegration feels like chaos because the nervous system is losing its previous map of reality.

Yet this dismantling is necessary for renewal. The old self its habits, assumptions, and fears must dissolve to make room for a more integrated pattern. It is not breakdown; it is reorganization.

In neuroscience, this process parallels **synaptic pruning.** During adolescence or major life transitions, the brain eliminates old connections to strengthen essential ones. The result is higher efficiency and coherence. To the conscious mind, it feels like loss forgetfulness, confusion, fatigue. To the deeper intelligence, it is optimization.

So when your life feels like it's "clearing out," it may literally be doing so. Circuits emotional, neural, relational are being pruned for clarity.

The Storm as Recalibration

Imagine a storm at sea. To the sailor, waves appear chaotic, hostile, without pattern. But viewed from above from the satellite or the divine vantage currents, wind systems, and gravitational fields form an elegant equation.

In human life, storms are not punishments. They are recalibrations energy redistributing itself to restore equilibrium. When we cling to what is familiar, even when it no longer serves us, God allows the storm to loosen our grip. The wind does not destroy the vessel; it turns it toward destiny.

The storm is divine mathematics correcting trajectory.

Shattered Glass and Galaxies

When glass breaks, it seems like pure destruction sharp edges, irreparable fragments. Yet under magnification, the cracks follow fractal geometry, echoing the branching of lightning or rivers. Even in fragmentation, there is pattern.

Human experience mirrors this. When life shatters, it rarely returns to its old shape but the pieces form a mosaic, reflecting more light than the original surface ever could.

Galaxies themselves were born from cosmic collapse. Massive stars exploded into supernovae, scattering elements that later condensed into new suns, planets, and life. Without collapse, there would be no creation.

The same energy that breaks a star births a world.

The Neuroscience of Reorganization

Stress is not merely emotional; it is neurological construction in progress. When we face chaos, the brain's **amygdala** signals alarm, releasing cortisol and adrenaline to ensure survival. But when stress persists, another process begins: the brain rewires itself to adapt.

Neuroscientists call this **adaptive plasticity.** Synapses that no longer serve are dismantled; new pathways form. This is not a gentle process. It can feel like exhaustion, brain fog, even despair. But biologically, it is progress your nervous system shedding obsolete architecture.

The prefrontal cortex, responsible for perspective and planning, strengthens once the turbulence settles. The mind gains clarity not despite chaos but through it.

This is why periods of confusion often precede sudden insight. The system destabilizes before reconfiguring to a higher order a pattern identical to chaotic systems in physics.

The Faith Within Fractals

Faith is the ability to trust the unseen geometry. When you cannot make sense of your circumstances, faith whispers: *There is order here, even if you can't yet read it.*

Consider the process of digital images. When viewed too closely, they dissolve into pixels dots of meaningless color. Step back, and the full picture emerges.

The same applies to divine design. Up close, life looks fragmented; from a higher distance, it reveals symmetry.

The faithful mind doesn't need to understand every detail it only needs to know that the design exists.

Story 1: The Detour

Naomi was a concert violinist whose life revolved around performance. When an accident injured her wrist, her career ended overnight. Years of training evaporated in seconds. "I felt discarded," she said. "Like everything I'd worked for had been erased."

During recovery, she began teaching beginners something she once considered beneath her skill. Over time, she discovered joy in explaining technique, in watching others grow. A decade later, she founded a music academy that transformed hundreds of young musicians.

She once believed the accident had ruined her purpose; later she realized it had expanded it. What seemed like chaos was architecture the rearrangement of identity to house a greater calling.

Story 2: The Collapse That Aligned

Daniel, a small business owner, lost everything during an economic downturn. Debt, betrayal, and foreclosure left him questioning his faith. "I kept praying for a sign," he recalled, "but all I got was silence."

In desperation, he moved to another city and took a modest job at a logistics firm humbling but stable. Within a year, he was promoted to operations manager. The systems he built during his time as a struggling entrepreneur became the foundation of his success.

Looking back, he said, "If my old company hadn't fallen apart, I'd still be living in anxiety, chasing something that didn't fit me."

His chaos was choreography. Loss was not punishment but redirection.

The Divine Geometry of Unfolding

In chaos theory, a system may appear unstable until it reaches a state called **self-organization** when order spontaneously emerges from disorder. Snowflakes crystallize from vapor, flocks of birds form synchronized patterns without a leader, neurons fire in rhythmic waves to produce thought.

Every act of manifestation passes through this threshold. What you perceive as "falling apart" is the moment before self-organization. The field must first lose its old pattern to make room for the new one.

Spiritually, this is the dark night of the soul the space between endings and beginnings where divine intelligence rearranges matter and meaning.

The Architecture Under Construction

God's design operates like fractal mathematics: repeating patterns across every scale of existence. The spiral of galaxies mirrors the shell of a snail. The branching of neurons mirrors lightning in a storm. Nothing is random.

When your life feels chaotic, you are inside the equation, too close to see its form. The design is still computing.

Chaos is not God's absence but His architecture under construction.

Seeing Through Higher Resolution

One day, when perspective expands, the randomness that tormented you will reveal symmetry. You will trace the line from loss to lesson, from detour to destiny, from collapse to creation. The connections will be too precise to deny.

The same force that governs galaxies governs your path. What appears as disorder is divine mathematics beyond current comprehension.

You are not lost inside chaos; you are being recalibrated by it.

Closing Reflection

Every storm, every fracture, every unexpected ending belongs to a greater equation. When the mind cries "random," the soul whispers "pattern."

Chaos is not destruction; it is divine rearrangement. It is the unrecognizable face of order in transit.

And one day, when clarity sharpens, you will see that every seeming accident, every unanswered prayer, every broken sequence aligned into perfect symmetry.

Because what you call chaos is precision beyond your current resolution.

What you call disorder is creation folding itself into new form.
And what you call loss is the law of hidden order God's architecture revealing itself, one fractal of faith at a time.

Chapter 11 – The Law of the Silent Signal: How Subconscious Frequencies Speak Louder Than Words

by Aria Vale

Before language, there was resonance. Before thought, there was vibration. Creation itself began not with speech, but with frequency the hum of divine intention moving through formlessness. Every word we speak, every gesture we make, is a surface ripple of deeper electromagnetic patterns that never stop transmitting.

The universe, like a finely tuned instrument, does not respond to what we say we want; it responds to what we *are*. The field listens to frequency, not vocabulary. Manifestation, at its highest level, is not a dialogue of words but an exchange of resonance.

The Hidden Language of the Body

Your heart is not only a pump. It is an electrical oscillator, generating the largest measurable electromagnetic field of any organ in the human body. According to research from the **HeartMath Institute**, this field extends several feet beyond the skin and synchronizes with others nearby. When two people are in proximity, their heart rhythms can harmonize, like tuning forks vibrating in shared frequency.

What we call "intuition," "vibe," or "atmosphere" is often this field-level communication. The nervous system reads subtle electromagnetic cues long before logic engages. Studies in **neurocardiology** reveal that the heart sends more signals to the brain than the brain sends to the heart meaning emotional states shape cognition before thoughts even form.

This is the silent signal the subconscious language through which all beings interact. You do not need to speak faith to radiate it. The body itself becomes the prayer.

The Science of Resonance

Resonance occurs when one system vibrates in harmony with another. In physics, two pendulums placed on the same beam eventually swing in unison. In acoustics, a tuning fork can cause another nearby fork of the same frequency to vibrate without physical contact.

Human beings function the same way. The electromagnetic frequencies of emotion and intention entrain others' fields through subtle resonance. When your internal state is coherent when heart, brain, and nervous system oscillate in unified rhythm you emit stability. People feel it. They may not know why they trust you, follow you, or calm around you, but their biology recognizes coherence.

Mirror neurons in the brain further amplify this process. These specialized cells activate both when you act and when you observe someone else acting, allowing emotional states to transfer silently between people. This is why peace can spread through a room as tangibly as panic. The signal is contagious.

Subconscious Transmission

The conscious mind speaks in sentences; the subconscious speaks in atmosphere. It broadcasts continuously through posture, microexpression, tone, breath, and electromagnetic field. Every suppressed emotion fear, shame, resentment remains stored as somatic vibration.

You can declare abundance a thousand times, but if your nervous system hums with scarcity, that is the frequency the field receives. You can pray for love, but if your body contracts in self-protection, the signal of fear overrides the words.

This is not moral judgment; it is electromagnetic fact. The subconscious governs about 95 percent of our daily behavior. It runs the patterns of safety, belonging, and expectation that shape experience long before thought intervenes. Words become powerless when the underlying vibration contradicts them.

The work of manifestation, then, is not to repeat stronger affirmations but to refine the signal to bring emotion, thought, and physiology into resonance with what is true, not merely desired.

The Emotional Frequency Spectrum

Each emotion corresponds to a measurable physiological state. Gratitude, compassion, and love produce coherent heart rhythms smooth, sine-wave patterns associated with efficient energy use and mental clarity. Fear and anger, by contrast, generate erratic, incoherent patterns that fragment focus and drain vitality.

HeartMath's research demonstrates that coherent states synchronize brain waves with the heart's rhythm, improving perception and decision-making. The more coherent your internal rhythm, the clearer your external results.

This is why peace attracts opportunity. Coherence communicates safety to the field. It tells the universe, *I am ready to receive.*

The Tuning Fork of Intention

Imagine two tuning forks — one represents your conscious desire, the other your subconscious state. When they vibrate at the same frequency, the sound amplifies; manifestation accelerates. When they differ, dissonance cancels the signal.

Most people attempt to manifest by striking the first fork — the conscious mind — louder. They repeat affirmations, visualize, and speak declarations. But if the second fork — the subconscious — remains tuned to fear, self-doubt, or guilt, the combined vibration cancels itself.

Alignment requires re-tuning, not shouting. It requires the slow work of emotional honesty, forgiveness, and nervous system regulation. The tuning process is invisible, but once resonance is achieved, movement becomes effortless.

Frequency Precedes Form

Long before words leave your mouth, the frequency of belief has already broadcast your message. The same law operates in prayer. Scripture records the divine phrase: *"Before you call, I will answer."* That is not poetic metaphor; it is a description of quantum responsiveness. The field registers vibration before articulation.

Faith is not convincing the universe to act; it is synchronizing with the frequency on which the answer already exists. You cannot pray for peace while radiating anxiety and expect coherence. The signal must match the desired reality.

In this sense, prayer, manifestation, and meditation are all calibration rituals means of bringing inner vibration into alignment with divine frequency. Words are secondary. The heart's electromagnetic broadcast is primary.

The Psychological Mirror

Every interaction is an energetic mirror reflecting the frequency you carry. The world responds not to personality but to pattern. People who live in chronic fear often find confirmation of it. Those who dwell in quiet confidence encounter cooperation and ease.

Psychology explains this through **pattern detection**: the brain's tendency to notice evidence that confirms existing belief. But spiritually, it's resonance: your subconscious signal organizes reality around its frequency.

Suppressed emotion becomes environmental architecture. The anger you deny appears as conflict; the love you withhold manifests as absence. The signal does not moralize it simply mirrors.

Change the signal, and the mirror rearranges.

Story 1: The Interview

Elena, a marketing executive, came to me after losing multiple job offers at the final stage. "I do everything right," she said. "I prepare, I perform well, but something always falls apart at the end."

We explored her internal state during interviews. Beneath her professionalism, she carried fear of judgment and the subtle belief that she was "impostor material." That anxiety, though invisible, pulsed through tone, microexpressions, and energy.

Instead of rehearsing scripts, she practiced heart coherence meditation slowing breath, recalling gratitude, stabilizing emotion before each meeting. The next interview felt "peaceful rather than pressured," she said.

She received the offer that same week. "It wasn't that I convinced them," she realized. "It's that I stopped defending myself."

Her silent signal shifted from fear to authenticity. The field responded accordingly.

Story 2: The Call Unsent

Marcus had been estranged from his father for years. They shared polite texts on holidays but nothing more. One night, after reading about heart coherence, he decided not to call but to simply sit and breathe, holding genuine forgiveness in his mind.

He later told me, "I didn't plan to reach out I just felt done with the resentment."

The next morning, his father called him unexpectedly, saying he'd "had a feeling" to reconnect.

Such moments are not coincidence. They are resonance made visible two signals finding coherence across distance.

The Lighthouse Signal

A lighthouse does not shout instructions to ships; it emits light in steady rhythm. The ocean interprets that rhythm as guidance. Likewise, manifestation does not depend on verbal command but on the stability of your inner frequency.

When your emotional field radiates coherence, you become a lighthouse in the fog of human noise. People, opportunities, and synchronicities orient toward you naturally not because you summoned them, but because you illuminated resonance.

The signal does not persuade; it attracts through precision.

The Art of Calibration

To refine your silent signal is not to chase positivity. It is to create coherence.

Begin not with affirmation but with observation. Notice how your body feels when you speak your goals. Do your shoulders tense? Does your breath shorten? The body reveals the true frequency beneath words.

Then bring attention to the heart. Slow the breath until rhythm steadies. Recall a moment of genuine appreciation. This shifts heart rate variability into coherence a measurable physiological alignment between heart and brain. Hold that feeling while contemplating your intention.

In this state, you are broadcasting a clean signal. No pleading, no grasping just resonance.

Over time, this coherence becomes habitual. The subconscious reprograms through repetition of peace. You begin to live as the frequency you once sought.

Words vs. Vibration

Words are surface ripples on the ocean of energy. They carry meaning only when propelled by coherent emotion. Empty affirmation without alignment is static sound without signal.

This is why many prayers and manifestations fail: the words request one reality while the vibration declares another. The field answers the vibration. Always.

Faith does not need eloquence. It requires purity of frequency thought, emotion, and body vibrating as one.

The Divine Receiver

The universe is not deaf; it is discerning. It decodes vibration, not volume. Divine intelligence operates like a radio tuned to frequency, not language. When your signal stabilizes in coherence, creation responds instantly not as favor, but as physics.

Every answered prayer begins as resonance, not request.

This is the meaning of *"Before you call, I will answer."* The call was never verbal. It was vibrational.

Final Reflection

All manifestation is communication. But the conversation is silent.

Your subconscious frequency speaks continuously through heartbeat, breath, and electromagnetic rhythm. Every thought that harmonizes or contradicts that rhythm refines the signal.

You do not attract by demand; you align by design.

When the heart's field becomes coherent, when the nervous system rests in peace, when emotion and intention vibrate in unison, your presence becomes fluent in the universe's native language.

Real manifestation makes no sound. It requires no argument, no persuasion. It is the quiet certainty that radiates from alignment a frequency so steady that reality cannot help but echo it.

In the end, you do not manifest by declaration but by calibration.

When your inner signal becomes pure enough, the field of God that silent intelligence permeating everything recognizes itself within you and responds as one continuous resonance.

That is the law of the silent signal: the revelation that the universe has never been listening to your words. It has always been listening to your *frequency*.

Chapter 12 – The Law of Collapse: The Fall Before Freedom

by Aria Vale

There is a moment when everything you built begins to dissolve. The strategies, affirmations, rituals, and identities that once gave shape to meaning lose their gravity. You call it breakdown. Heaven calls it accuracy.

You cannot ascend until what was false in you collapses. Every structure built from fear must fail, not as punishment but as correction. The fall is the last act of mercy the moment when illusion can no longer hold the weight of consciousness.

The Fall Before Freedom

People think awakening feels like light. It begins more like fire. What burns is not the world but the scaffolding of self the false architecture constructed to protect from uncertainty. You lose control, and in the absence of control, you meet reality naked.

The collapse is revelation. When the surface shatters, what remains is structural truth what can survive the absence of pretense.

The Psychological Breakdown

When identity disintegrates, the nervous system interprets it as danger. Dopamine drops. The prefrontal cortex loses dominance, the limbic system surges, and the mind enters withdrawal from certainty. The collapse is not moral crisis; it is **neurobiological surrender**.

The brain clings to patterns of predictability because prediction equals safety. When those patterns fail, the chemical loops that sustained ego dissolve. The result is a hollowing out confusion, disorientation, fatigue. This is not malfunction; it is detox.

Trauma research shows that after meaning collapses, the brain undergoes **neural rewiring**. Synaptic connections associated with control and expectation weaken. New circuits slower, quieter, more perceptive begin to form. The old identity dies chemically before it dies conceptually.

In psychological terms, this is **identity fragmentation**. In spiritual terms, it is death before resurrection.

The Spiritual Mechanics

"Whoever loses his life shall find it." The collapse fulfills this line with clinical precision. The ego prays for rescue; God responds with dismantling.

The divine does not comfort the false self; it removes it. Every prayer for transformation is a request for destruction disguised as hope. Collapse is divine surgery removing the infection of illusion without anesthesia.

The instruments of dismantling are rarely dramatic. They are silence, loss, endings that make no sense, prayers that return unanswered. The ego calls it abandonment. Spirit calls it procedure.

No guru can stop it. No ritual can soften it. Grace does not negotiate with illusion. It removes what cannot remain.

The Death of Self-Help

The self-help industry teaches that brokenness can be fixed through steps, tools, and better affirmations. But what is collapsing in you cannot be managed it must be surrendered. The method cannot save what was never real.

The manifestation world confuses creation with control. It sells optimism to minds addicted to certainty. Collapse destroys that addiction. It shows that you never manifested anything; you only aligned temporarily with what was already written.

You don't need more steps. You need fewer lies.

When the scaffolding of self-improvement falls, what remains is raw awareness no longer trying to become divine, simply recognizing it.

Story 1: The Unbuilding

Lara spent years teaching corporate leadership seminars about mindset and success. When her company collapsed, she lost her job, her savings, and her sense of authority. For months, she could not read the same books she once quoted. The words felt sterile, rehearsed.

She described that season as "silence that wouldn't end." Eventually, she stopped trying to fix the silence. She sat inside it.

"I realized," she told me later, "everything I taught was a performance to avoid this feeling. Now that it's here, I'm free."

Nothing replaced her identity. It simply dissolved. In the emptiness, perception returned not empowerment, but clarity.

Story 2: The Burned Foundation

Adrian built his life around control. Business, health, spiritual practice everything was planned, tracked, optimized. Then his father died unexpectedly. Every system failed. He couldn't meditate, couldn't work, couldn't think. He called it failure.

Months later, something shifted. He began noticing simple things the sound of traffic, the rhythm of his breath. He stopped performing stability and started experiencing reality.

He once said, "I lost faith in manifestation. I gained faith in truth."

That was the real transformation the collapse of dependency on control disguised as spirituality.

The Biology of Emptiness

After collapse, the body enters a state resembling dormancy. Brain scans of individuals emerging from identity disruption show **deactivation of the default mode network** the region responsible for self-referential thought. When this network quiets, perception expands. The mind stops narrating and begins witnessing.

Cortisol levels stabilize. Breathing deepens. The parasympathetic system the "rest and restore" mechanism takes over. The organism rebuilds not through activity, but through stillness.

This emptiness is not death; it is **data reorganization**. The psyche recalibrates around truth, stripping away symbolic noise. The feeling of "nothing left" is the nervous system resetting its baseline.

You are not being erased. You are being reformatted.

The Unmaking as Creation

Truth cannot coexist with the illusion that someone else will save you. Collapse removes intermediaries the comforting idols of technique, philosophy, and performance.

When you are stripped of every tool, only awareness remains. That awareness is not personal; it is structural the same intelligence that keeps stars from colliding and cells from mutating. You have never been separate from it. You only built narratives that obscured it.

The unmaking is creation in its most honest form: nothing added, only falsehood removed.

When the ego burns, the eternal breathes through the ashes.

Final Reflection

The collapse is not the end of you. It is the end of everything that wasn't.

No one can save you because what you are cannot die.

The fall before freedom is the mercy of reality the final gesture of a universe tired of pretending for your comfort.

The illusion burns. The truth remains, silent and indestructible.

Chapter 13 – The Law of the Hollow World: How Modern Life Kills the Soul

by Aria Vale

Humanity built cities to escape the cold and the wild. Yet in doing so, it caged itself inside a synthetic paradise. The walls gleam. The floors shine. Everything hums with precision. But beneath the hum, something vital has gone silent.

We built cities for comfort, and in doing so, buried our souls beneath concrete.

Modern life simulates safety while draining vitality. The noise of progress covers the absence of meaning. Every structure that promises convenience carries a hidden cost: disconnection. The ancient chaos of nature was dangerous, but it kept the human spirit alive. Now, surrounded by glass and signal, people move through controlled climates, controlled conversations, controlled emotions and call it freedom.

Digital Colonization of Consciousness

The body still walks in the twenty-first century, but the mind has been captured by the screen.

Social media, algorithms, and notifications function as an invisible empire a system that harvests human attention as currency. Dopamine spikes, then crashes. The prefrontal cortex, responsible for focus and long-term vision, dims under constant stimulation. Neural scans show inhibition in the same regions that weaken in addiction.

We are connected to everything except ourselves.

Each scroll is a microdose of validation. Each click is an impulse reinforced by machine learning. The nervous system, designed for depth and slow perception, now fires in fragments. The human brain, once capable of hours of contemplation, has been trained to live in eight-second intervals.

Reward-loop exhaustion replaces fulfillment. The cycle of stimulus and fatigue keeps people restless but passive.

The system does not need to imprison the body when it has colonized the mind.

The Spiritual Mechanism of Numbness

Feeling has become dangerous in a culture that profits from distraction.

People no longer pray; they refresh. They no longer meditate; they scroll. Silence has become unbearable because silence reveals the truth of how empty they have become.

The devil no longer appears as darkness. He appears as infinite scrolling.

Pleasure replaces presence. Consumption replaces contemplation. The entertainment feed has become a synthetic version of transcendence endless stimulation without elevation.

Emotional anesthesia has become lifestyle. People escape pain so effectively that they also escape meaning. To avoid silence is to avoid God, because God speaks only through stillness.

The Death of Presence

To be human once meant to exist inside rhythms dawn and dusk, planting and harvest, rest and labor. Now time is fluorescent and continuous. The planet spins through cycles, but modern life ignores them.

Artificial light abolishes night. Work continues without season. Sleep becomes optional, intimacy optional, reflection optional.

"What does it profit a man to gain the world and lose his soul?"

Presence has been traded for productivity. People live as units of output, measured by metrics that never end. They mistake activity for existence, motion for meaning.

To be unreachable was once a sign of solitude. Now it is rebellion.

The Biology of Disconnection

The decay of the soul begins in the body.

Chronic cortisol elevation from constant digital exposure keeps the nervous system in low-grade fight-or-flight. Blue light suppresses melatonin, eroding REM sleep the phase where memory and emotion integrate. Serotonin depletes in those who rarely see sunlight or move their bodies.

We evolved for sunlight and silence. We now live under neon and noise.

Urban design amplifies isolation: high-density proximity without intimacy, countless faces without recognition. The nervous system, unable to process constant novelty, retreats into numbness. Depression becomes adaptation the body's way of conserving energy in an environment it cannot regulate.

This is not malfunction. It is rebellion.

The body resists a world that denies its nature.

A Modern Case: The Perfect Life

Elias lived in a tower of glass. His apartment was immaculate: minimalist furniture, filtered air, quiet automation. He had a six-figure income, biometric trackers, weekly therapy, and no reason to complain.

Every metric confirmed success. Yet at night, when the lights dimmed and the city's hum turned low, he felt a steady sense of absence. He would unlock his phone out of habit, open and close apps without purpose, searching for something unnamed.

One evening, he stood before his floor-to-ceiling window, watching identical buildings glow against the dark. He realized he could see hundreds of apartments, but no faces. Only light.

Surrounded by brilliance, he lived in interior darkness.

That recognition did not free him. It simply made him honest.

The Soul's Weak Signal

When every form of pleasure stops working, the soul begins to whisper.

Emptiness is not failure; it is data returning to silence. The system's hypnosis breaks not through enlightenment, but through exhaustion. When stimulation ceases to numb, the individual begins to feel again faintly at first, like a weak radio signal under static.

The feeling is unfamiliar, almost painful: boredom, longing, grief without story. This is not depression. It is the reactivation of sensitivity. The human instrument tuning itself back to reality.

The return of depth begins as discomfort.

The Path Back

There is no system to escape the system. Only subtraction.

The soul does not recover through more knowledge or higher vibration. It recovers through absence of screens, noise, performance, and ambition.

You don't escape the system by fighting it. You leave by remembering you were never built for it.

Silence is not a practice. It is the native language of consciousness. Stillness is not technique; it is alignment with design.

Presence begins where stimulation ends. Reconnection begins where consumption dies.

Those who rediscover God do so not through belief but through the long withdrawal from distraction.

Closing Lines

The modern world is full, yet the soul starves.

People move faster, speak louder, and live longer yet fewer know why.

Until you unplug from the noise, you will never hear God again.

Chapter 14 – The Law of Withdrawal: The Power of Disappearing from the System

by Aria Vale

The modern human lives in constant exposure. Everything is visible, recorded, and indexed movement, speech, preference, emotion. The private self has become a relic. To exist now means to be observed.

In the age of exposure, invisibility has become the last freedom.

The nervous system was never designed for continuous observation. Visibility keeps the body in subtle fight-or-flight cortisol elevated, heart rate vigilant, posture unconsciously defensive. When identity is watched, it performs. What performs cannot feel. The organism becomes a brand, and the person behind it disappears.

The Age of Overexposure

Social platforms transformed survival instinct into performance instinct. The tribe once guaranteed safety through belonging; now belonging is simulated through attention. A post becomes a pulse — proof of continued existence.

But to be seen endlessly is to lose texture. When the gaze never lifts, the interior collapses. The mind begins to think for the audience, not for itself. Every opinion is pre-edited, every gesture optimized for engagement. Authenticity becomes impossible under surveillance.

Chronic visibility fragments consciousness. The nervous system, overstimulated by micro-judgment and constant self-monitoring, develops the same symptoms found in social anxiety and trauma. The brain, flooded with social data, cannot distinguish real threat from imagined scrutiny. The result is exhaustion disguised as relevance.

The Myth of Relevance

Modernity equates visibility with worth. To matter means to be searchable. Silence is interpreted as failure.

The modern soul would rather be noticed than free.

Relevance is the new religion — measured in metrics, likes, and impressions. The more a person broadcasts, the less they exist. Constant self-presentation divides attention into mirrors: who you are, who you seem, who you hope they think you are.

Algorithms amplify this dependence. Validation triggers the dopamine loop. Absence produces withdrawal. The self becomes a performer trapped in the audience's applause.

Every click promises recognition but delivers captivity.

The Neurobiology of Withdrawal

When a person steps out of the circuit, the brain begins to repair itself.

Dopamine cycles flatten. The prefrontal cortex responsible for discipline and decision regains control from the limbic drive of novelty seeking. The **default-mode network**, suppressed by overstimulation, reactivates, allowing the mind to retrieve memory, reflect, and form independent thought.

Attention stabilizes. Time slows.

Silence is sensory fasting a detox for perception. The absence of input forces the nervous system to re-regulate. Sleep deepens, cortisol drops, immune response normalizes. What feels like boredom is neurological healing.

Withdrawal restores sovereignty over perception. The organism stops reacting and starts perceiving again.

Disappearance as Discipline

To disappear consciously is not abandonment. It is correction.

Withdrawal is not collapse but choice a refusal to keep negotiating with noise. When you remove yourself from the system's tempo, you encounter the natural tempo of thought.

History has always preserved a few who vanished deliberately: monks, hermits, writers, scientists, ascetics. They are not saints but evidence. Distance restores cognition.

Noise compresses intelligence into reflex. Silence expands it into comprehension.

To withdraw is not to reject the world but to see it without distortion.

The Psychological Detox

The first symptom of withdrawal is guilt. Modern conditioning equates presence with productivity. In absence, the system whispers failure. You will feel agitation, restlessness, then boredom.

Boredom is not emptiness. It is withdrawal symptom from overstimulation.

The nervous system, used to constant input, panics in stillness. It interprets quiet as threat. But if you remain, the panic dissolves into clarity. The body relearns neutrality. The mind remembers what undirected thought feels like.

After the detox, perception sharpens. Internal silence becomes less absence and more atmosphere a field in which things regain proportion.

The Spiritual Mechanics of Vanishing

When the noise fades, reality stops being symbolic and becomes real.

Colors return to their true brightness. Faces reveal fatigue and beauty simultaneously. The ordinary regains gravity. Nothing mystical occurs; interference simply ends.

Withdrawal reclaims the original architecture of perception the unmediated relationship between self and world. Sensation becomes fact rather than entertainment.

You begin to hear again, not the metaphoric "inner voice," but the physical hum of existence unfiltered by commentary. Awareness resumes its natural function: direct experience without narrative.

Story Fragment

A man deleted every account, left the city, and moved into a cabin by a lake. The first week, he woke repeatedly at night, reaching for a phone that no longer existed. His mind searched for an audience that wasn't there.

He described panic at the absence of verification. The silence felt hostile.

After a month, he stopped measuring days. He noticed that thoughts began arriving fully formed, without external prompt. He said, "I don't feel happy. I just feel *here*."

He did not call it enlightenment. He called it recovery.

The Law of Strategic Invisibility

Every organism in nature withdraws cyclically. Trees retreat in winter. Animals hibernate. Even the heart alternates between contraction and rest. Life depends on rhythm, not permanence of display.

If you never disappear, you never evolve.

Human beings abandoned the rhythm of absence. They replaced rest with exposure, renewal with continuity. Constant availability destroys internal regeneration.

Strategic invisibility is biological hygiene a phase of metabolic, emotional, and cognitive reset. Without it, perception dulls. With it, intelligence refines.

The refusal to withdraw is not productivity; it is decay.

The Paradox of Return

Withdrawal is not exile. It is calibration.

When you re-enter the world after silence, you no longer seek attention. You move through the environment without broadcasting. The noise of others does not recruit your nervous system.

You observe without absorbing. Influence begins only after indifference to visibility.

The point of withdrawal is not escape but re-entry without noise.

Presence, once freed from the need to be seen, becomes substance again.

Closing Reflection

The system teaches you to exist through exposure, but exposure is erosion.

You are not here to be seen. You are here to see.

Disappear long enough for the system to forget you and for your soul to remember itself.

Chapter 15 – The Law of the Inner Architecture: How Thought Becomes Structure

by Aria Vale

Reality does not bend to wishful thinking. It reorganizes according to structure.

Every consistent belief functions as a construction code an internal architecture that determines what you perceive, how you react, and which possibilities register as real.

The world doesn't form around what you wish. It forms around what you repeatedly assume.

Thought is not ornamental decoration layered on top of experience. It is the blueprint that instructs the brain what to build. The mind is not a painter; it is an engineer of perception.

The Invisible Blueprint

Each human being moves through the same external world, but not the same internal architecture. The nervous system filters billions of signals per second, selecting only what matches its existing model of reality. What you call "the world" is that filtered remainder.

Belief acts as the invisible scaffold. A person convinced that life is hostile perceives threat in neutral expressions, tone, or chance events. Another, structured around trust, walks through the same stimuli but reads cooperation. The difference is not event but architecture.

Manifestation, stripped of mysticism, is the gradual translation of thought into biological wiring.

The Cognitive Mechanics of Construction

Modern neuroscience describes the brain as a **predictive coding system**. It does not record reality; it forecasts it. Incoming data are constantly compared against internal models predictions built from memory, emotion, and repetition.

Perception, therefore, is a negotiation between expectation and evidence. Most of what you "see" is prediction confirmed. When beliefs remain stable long enough, the brain deprioritizes contradictions and privileges coherence. Contradictory facts fade into statistical noise.

This is how architecture solidifies. Reality stops debating you. It complies with your model.

Neuroplasticity underwrites the process: neural pathways that fire together wire together. The stronger the pattern, the harder it becomes to question. Manifestation is not a miracle; it is prediction bias encoded in tissue.

The Embodiment Loop

Thought becomes visible through the body. A single assumption triggers emotion, which alters physiology heart rate, tone, microexpression, muscle tension. These shifts communicate silently, inviting reciprocal behavior from others.

A person expecting rejection stiffens slightly, voice tightening. The listener senses discomfort, withdraws, and confirms the prediction. The architecture deepens.

"You live inside architecture made of recurring signals."

Emotion completes the loop. Repeated enough, this cycle carves identity into posture and tone. Over time, the structure builds itself into physical space: the friends you attract, the environments you tolerate, the choices you justify.

Belief is not an idea in the head. It is an ecosystem sustained by feedback.

The Architecture of Expectation

Expectation is not fantasy; it is a survival function. The brain saves energy by predicting what will happen next. Each expectation is an architectural shortcut, reducing uncertainty.

When expectation collapses through trauma, loss, or betrayal the architecture fractures. The nervous system scrambles to rebuild coherence. This is why disorientation feels unbearable: the map has dissolved, and raw data rushes in without filter.

Transformation requires rebuilding prediction from new principles. Real change is not a surge of motivation; it is sustained redesign. The nervous system adapts to consistency, not intensity.

The Error Signal

Between belief and reality lies the **prediction error** the difference between what you expected and what occurred. When the error is small, the brain corrects easily. When it is large, identity trembles.

Most people resolve this discomfort by distortion: they reinterpret reality to preserve the old model. This is cognitive dissonance architecture defending itself from renovation.

The wise do the opposite. They allow collapse. They let the model fail so a more accurate one can be built.

This is the hidden cost of growth dismantling the mental scaffolding that once guaranteed stability.

The error signal is not punishment. It is instruction.

The Psychological Architecture

The psyche is not abstract. It is spatial. You live inside a mental building composed of memories, habits, and self-concepts. Every identity forms a room. Fear occupies one corridor. Ambition occupies another. Some doors have not been opened in years.

These rooms determine movement. Even when circumstances change, you navigate the same interior layout. This is why external success rarely feels different the building remains the same.

Transformation is architectural, not ornamental. It begins with demolition, not decoration.

You are not creating reality. You are renovating perception.

Story Fragment

Leah grew up in scarcity. Even after earning more than enough to live comfortably, she checked her bank account daily, anxious without reason. Her body still behaved as if collapse were imminent.

Therapy, education, and logic changed little until she began observing her own architecture: the predictive model of "there will never be enough." She practiced noticing safety rather than danger meals, shelter, consistent income. Gradually, her nervous system learned new parameters.

Months later, she described the shift simply: "I stopped waiting for loss."

Her external situation hadn't changed. Her internal architecture had. Reality followed the new design because perception finally allowed it.

Neural Blueprint Renewal

The human brain is plastic malleable by repetition and emotion. Studies show that new neural pathways form through sustained focus and relevance. What we repeat, we reinforce; what we neglect, we dismantle.

Each consistent thought is a blueprint submitted to biology. Over time, the brain memorizes the pattern, delegating it to automation. Identity becomes muscle memory.

What people call "manifesting" is simply **consistent signal integration** the merging of mental rehearsal and emotional confirmation until the body treats the imagined as ordinary. The world then reflects this familiarity because perception stops resisting it.

The organism always returns to what feels architecturally true.

The Principle of Design Integrity

Faith is not belief in miracles. It is fidelity to a blueprint not yet materialized.

The divine does not reward emotion; it mirrors structure. When inner order aligns with factual coherence not wishful thinking, but logical stability outcomes converge without effort.

Chaos is not external. It is internal misalignment between structure and signal. When thought, emotion, and behavior follow the same design, resistance ends because contradiction has no architecture to sustain it.

Inner architecture is not metaphysical; it is mechanical. The universe is a system that responds to consistent parameters.

Spiritual Minimalism

The mature mind does not chase manifestations. It builds frameworks.

Each belief is a beam. Each emotion is mortar. Each habit is stone. Over time, these materials harden into lived reality. Remove one element and the structure shifts. Replace enough, and the entire world changes orientation.

Creation is silent construction. The laws do not require belief only design accuracy.

You do not manifest by wanting. You manifest by constructing.

Build carefully. Because you live inside what you think.

Chapter 16 – The Law of Friction: Make the Right Thing Inevitable

by Aria Vale

Motivation is fragile. Friction is permanent.
What you repeatedly do has less to do with willpower and more to do with the path your system has made easiest to follow.

When two options compete, the nervous system chooses the one with less resistance. That pull is **behavioral gravity** the invisible force that decides whether you scroll or study, pray or postpone, act or avoid.

If your system makes the wrong choice easier, you will become the wrong choice.

Behavioral Gravity

The human organism is an energy economist. It avoids unnecessary expenditure. Between any two behaviors, it will fall toward the smoother gradient the route requiring fewer decisions, fewer movements, less effort.

Motivation spikes briefly but decays rapidly; friction persists. The environment, not enthusiasm, governs consistency.

You don't overcome gravity by inspiration. You alter the slope.

Choice Architecture 101

Every system you interact with — digital, physical, or social — carries *defaults*. Layout is law.

The placement of an object determines its likelihood of use. Visibility increases probability. Distance decreases it.

Designers call these **affordances** — the physical or digital cues that suggest action. Behavioral economists call them **nudges** when they help, **sludge** when they hinder. Both operate silently.

Your calendar, your notifications, your desk, and your kitchen function as choice architects. They script behavior without negotiation.

If the cookie jar is within arm's reach, consumption becomes default. If your running shoes sit by the door, motion becomes inevitable.

Micro-layout dictates macro-results.

The Neuroeconomics of Effort

The brain's primary constraint is metabolic. Prefrontal control planning, restraint, reasoning consumes high energy. Instinct and habit cost less.

Dopamine biases toward immediacy. The limbic system prioritizes fast, easy rewards. This is not moral weakness. It is evolutionary design.

The rule is simple: **Don't out-argue your biology. Out-design it.**

Reduce the effort for actions you want to repeat. Increase it for those you want to extinguish.

The nervous system will follow the path of least metabolic cost. You decide what that path is.

Friction Math

Small amounts of friction have exponential impact.

Adding **30–60 seconds** of delay kills most impulsive behaviors. Removing **30–60 seconds** from a desired one doubles adherence.

Examples:
— Move distraction apps into a folder behind two taps and a password.
— Preload your project file before bed so creation begins at the click of a key.

– Keep workout gear visible, paired, and unavoidable.
– Separate your phone from your workspace by physical distance — a single wall can save an hour.

Behavior modification is mechanical, not mystical.

Cue → Action → Reward (Clean Version)

Behavior runs on a loop: cue triggers action; action delivers reward. You don't break loops — you rewire them.

1. **Redesign the cue:** make the desired trigger visible, timed, and context-specific.

2. **Compress the action:** reduce steps; one-click start beats ten.

3. **Upgrade the reward:** attach immediate micro-wins — progress trackers, completion sound, visual streaks.

Consistency outweighs intensity. Friction compounds like interest; a 1% improvement in layout multiplies over months.

Environment Is Identity in Physical Form

Your environment broadcasts policy. It doesn't ask.

If your room contradicts your goals, your room will win.

A cluttered desk invites drift. A phone beside the bed guarantees delayed sleep. A workspace flooded with unrelated stimuli fractures attention.

Identity is a system expressed through design. You are not failing; your environment is succeeding at something else.

Shift from self-control to context control. Remove negotiation entirely.

Case Study

A writer struggled for months to maintain a daily habit. Each morning began with scrolling, then guilt.

One afternoon, he stripped his environment: cleared the desk, blocked non-writing websites, staged headphones and outline, and left his writing app open overnight.

The next morning, he sat down and began typing before thinking.

Forty-five minutes passed. Then another day. Then thirty consecutive days.

No surge of discipline only a reconfigured friction profile.

The system changed; behavior followed.

The Anti-Goal: Strategic Sludge

You can reverse-engineer temptation by adding resistance.

Distance: store indulgences far away or behind multiple steps.
Delay: add time-locks or mandatory wait periods.
Doubt: prompt reflection "Do you still want this in 10 minutes?"

For positive habits, invert these. Bring closer, faster, clearer.

Design success into reach; bury failure under effort.

The 48-Hour Friction Audit

Implementation is surgical:

1. **List** top three desired and top three undesired behaviors.
2. For each, **map** cue → action → reward.
3. **Remove one barrier (−30s)** for desired.
4. **Add one barrier (+30s)** for undesired.

5. **Stage** tomorrow's start state tonight tools, files, clothes.
6. **Lock one default:** calendar block, app blocker, auto-launch routine.
7. **Measure** adherence over 14 days by days executed, not output.

Systems are promises you make to your future nervous system.

Make It Inevitable

Willpower is a bridge. Friction is a road.

When the path of least resistance aligns with your intention, success becomes mechanical.

You no longer struggle toward better behavior. You slide into it.

When the wrong choice feels heavier, and the right one feels natural, manifestation ends. Engineering begins.

Chapter 17 – The Law of Systems: You Don't Rise to Goals, You Fall to Design

by Aria Vale

Goals feel powerful because they simulate progress. They offer instant clarity a short dopamine surge disguised as direction. Yet nothing in your environment changes when you set one. The calendar stays full. The habits stay intact. The mind returns to its baseline.

A goal changes nothing. A system changes everything that happens next.

The Mirage of Goals

Goals are emotional snapshots a vision of a future self projected by temporary motivation. They describe what you want, not how you'll consistently behave when that desire fades.

Motivation cannot survive friction, distraction, or time. It burns bright, then dies. Systems, by contrast, don't require enthusiasm. They function automatically once built.

Manifestation is not the act of imagining outcomes. It is the design of conditions that make those outcomes routine.

You never rise above the quality of your system. You default to it.

The Mechanics of Default Behavior

Roughly half of daily actions are automatic. They're not chosen; they're executed by neural scripts the brain conserves to save energy. The nervous system prefers predictability because uncertainty costs metabolic resources.

This means you manifest not through effort, but through automation. You are a walking sum of your current systems the patterns that repeat without negotiation.

When those systems contradict your stated goals, drift appears. You don't fail because you're weak. You fail because your infrastructure doesn't support the signal you're sending. Motivation without structure collapses under its own weight.

The Architecture of Systems

A functional system has four parts: **environment, triggers, process, and feedback.**

1. **Environment** defines what's easy, what's hard, what's visible.
2. **Triggers** initiate the behavior.
3. **Process** maintains the sequence once started.
4. **Feedback** corrects deviation.

Without feedback, all systems decay. Every stable system biological, digital, mechanical survives through correction loops. Without them, entropy wins.

Entropy and Drift

Behavioral entropy is silent. Routines decay invisibly. A single skipped task becomes habit erosion. Missed cues dissolve into disorganization. Chaos accumulates until what once worked no longer does.

The problem isn't lack of motivation. It's lack of maintenance.

Every structure, physical or behavioral, collapses when unobserved. The brain drifts toward comfort; the environment drifts toward clutter. Entropy is constant. Systems must evolve to counter it.

The Law of the Small Loop

The smaller the feedback loop, the faster the correction. This is the true engine of progress.

Most people review their data finances, habits, health too late to adapt. Feedback must be tight enough to inform the next cycle, not the next year.

Budget daily, not monthly. Adjust nutrition weekly, not seasonally. Evaluate productivity each night, not after burnout.

Reality doesn't reward effort. It rewards iteration speed.

Micro-corrections beat macro-resolutions. Systems with tight loops self-stabilize; those with lag disintegrate.

Identity as Operating System

Systems run on the operating system of identity. You can't execute high-efficiency design protocols on outdated self-concept software.

Identity provides default permissions: what you allow, tolerate, or pursue. When you upgrade identity, you reconfigure every process that depends on it.

You don't become disciplined. You become designed.

Behavior aligns not with aspiration but with self-definition. The moment the identity shifts from "trying" to "being," resistance drops.

Systems rewrite personality from the outside in.

Story Fragment

A product designer kept failing to maintain creative consistency. Each quarter, he vowed to "be more disciplined," but output stagnated.

Then he built a micro-system:
— one fixed writing block each morning;
— a pre-loaded template that opened on startup;
— an automation that silenced notifications.

After a month, his productivity tripled. He described the process as "effortless, almost mechanical." Motivation was irrelevant. The design carried him.

The emotional highs vanished, but so did the chaos.

The system became the source of flow.

System vs. Spiral

Poor systems create **negative feedback spirals** each small error multiplies through lack of correction. Great systems create **reinforcing loops** success compounds automatically.

A neglected workspace leads to distraction, missed work, guilt, and more avoidance a downward spiral. A clean workspace triggers clarity, early start, visible progress, positive feedback an upward spiral.

The difference is not attitude. It's loop design.

The brain follows the dominant spiral. The system determines which one prevails.

System Construction Protocol

Building a system is engineering, not affirmation.

1. **Define recurring conditions, not outcomes.** Replace "write a book" with "sit at the desk at 8:00 AM."

2. **Identify triggers.** Tie them to existing cues: after coffee, before leaving, at log-in.

3. **Automate repetition.** Use schedules, apps, or environment cues.

4. **Embed feedback.** Track daily metrics or reflection notes.

5. **Prune regularly.** Remove steps that create drag. Entropy never sleeps.

Your system is a living organism. It evolves or it decays.

When Design Becomes Destiny

Manifestation, viewed through systems, becomes self-regulation at scale. When your environment, schedule, and identity agree, the future stops resisting.

Discipline is replaced by infrastructure.
Faith becomes process fidelity.
Hope becomes calibration.

You no longer chase outcomes. You run a design that produces them.

You don't rise to your goals. You fall to your design and that's where your real life begins.

Chapter 18 – The Law of Integration: When All Systems Converge

by Aria Vale

At a certain point, self-improvement ends not because you have mastered control, but because control dissolves.

You stop alternating between opposing poles discipline and surrender, action and rest, noise and silence. The system stabilizes. The fragments merge.

Integration is not balance. It is the disappearance of conflict.

When every subsystem thought, body, routine, emotion operates in synchrony, effort vanishes. The machine no longer resists itself. The organism runs without drag. This is the moment of convergence: the shift from managing reality to embodying it.

The Moment of Convergence

Every transformation begins in pieces. You learn discipline, then rest. You study friction, then systems. You isolate each variable. But maturity begins when the boundaries between them dissolve.

At this stage, laws no longer compete. You don't "apply" rest or "force" discipline each arises naturally from timing. Movement and stillness become two aspects of one rhythm.

Integration is less about balance and more about coherence. Nothing is forced because nothing is divided.

The Physics of Coherence

Complex systems evolve toward synchronization. In neuroscience, synchronized neural oscillations signal efficient cognition. In ecosystems, species equilibrate into homeostasis. In orchestras, distinct instruments align into resonance.

When subsystems harmonize, waste disappears. Energy previously spent on internal correction converts into output.

Human performance follows the same principle. When identity, behavior, and environment operate under one code, no energy leaks into contradiction. The system's total efficiency rises exponentially not through motivation, but through order.

Manifestation becomes the natural consequence of internal engineering. The parts stop competing and start collaborating.

The End of the Fragmented Self

Fragmentation produces resistance. One self wants expansion; another clings to safety. One prays; another doubts. One plans; another avoids. Every contradiction splits the nervous system between incompatible commands.

When you integrate, the dualities dissolve. There is no "spiritual self" versus "practical self," no "manifesting self" versus "working self." The architecture stabilizes into one continuous identity.

When the self stops arguing with itself, the universe stops arguing back.

This is not harmony through control. It is the absence of internal noise. You cease performing dual roles and start living as a unified system.

The Biological Integration

Neuroscience describes this as synchronized efficiency: heart and brain rhythms align; prediction error decreases; neural coherence replaces hyperactivity.

During peak flow states, prefrontal inhibition lowers the inner critic quiets while sensory and motor networks synchronize. The body and environment operate as one circuit.

Integration feels like calm precision, not euphoria. Output increases even as effort disappears. It is not relaxation, but frictionless operation.

When all subsystems communicate perfectly, performance feels silent.

Systemic Harmony

Each prior principle was a subsystem preparing for this stage.

Action creates motion.
Resistance defines strength.
Rest consolidates learning.
Architecture provides form.
Friction refines pathways.
System sustains consistency.

Integration merges them. The process becomes self-regulating. You no longer "motivate" yourself because the environment, identity, and action cycle sustain one another automatically.

The system reaches equilibrium — dynamic, adaptive, alive.

Story Fragment

An architect once obsessed over optimization: morning routines, productivity trackers, diet cycles. Every law functioned in isolation. Yet his progress plateaued.

Then he stopped tracking and focused on design one system that contained everything: wake, walk, create, reflect, sleep. No intensity, just rhythm.

Months later, he reported breakthroughs   clarity in design, calm in decisions, precision in timing. "It feels," he said, "like something is working through me, not from me."

He had not achieved mastery. He had achieved integration.

The Collapse of Effort

Effort is the friction between subsystems. When the inner design aligns, that friction disappears.

Discipline turns to design; design turns to instinct.

Habits stop feeling practiced. They become anatomy. Rest is no longer earned; it arrives when needed. Focus is no longer forced; it follows flow.

This is not automation by apathy. It is automation by precision. You have tuned your systems so accurately that even stillness is productive.

The Law of Internal Synchrony

Integration is not achieved by adding more rules but by reducing interference. You don't need more control only less contradiction.

When the organism becomes self-correcting, feedback loops close seamlessly. Mistakes resolve without drama; corrections happen subconsciously. The body, mind, and environment act as one adaptive intelligence.

This is the threshold where "manifestation" ceases to be a verb. It becomes a property of being.

The Spiritual Reflection

If earlier chapters dealt with engineering, this one deals with emergence. Structure refines into order. Order refines into simplicity.

Integration is divine order expressed through human precision a perfect alignment between internal law and external pattern.

The creator and creation finally operate on the same frequency.

The Unified Field

Every stable system, once fully aligned, becomes self-perpetuating. It maintains itself through minimal correction.

At this stage, you are not applying principles   you are the principle.
You do not chase coherence   you radiate it.
You no longer manifest   you maintain creation by being it.

Chapter 19 – The Law of Perception Collapse: When Reality Stops Being Objective

by Aria Vale

When perception becomes exact enough, the external world begins to disappear.
Reality stops happening *to* you; it starts happening *through* you.

At this stage of integration, the distance between inner interpretation and outer event collapses. What once appeared as "objective" reveals itself as a projection stabilized by agreement, not absolute truth. Manifestation ceases to be the act of influencing external matter; it becomes perceptual engineering the reorganization of awareness itself.

The Collapse of Objectivity

The human brain never observes the world directly. Every sensation sight, sound, texture is a neural construction predicted from past experience. The senses deliver fragments; the brain renders coherence.

As integration deepens, the mind's predictive power grows so consistent that the illusion of separation begins to dissolve. The border between perception and environment becomes porous.

Objectivity, once worshiped as truth, is exposed as collective approximation.

What you call "reality" is a probability field resolved by expectation.

The Brain as a Reality-Rendering Engine

Neuroscience calls it *predictive coding*. The brain does not record data; it predicts what should be there, then updates only when surprised. The eyes receive light, but the mind supplies meaning.

Consider visual illusions: stationary images that appear to move, or colors that shift by context. The sensory data never changed   interpretation did. Hallucinations, placebo responses, psychosomatic healing   all examples of perception overriding physical input.

The body obeys the dominant prediction. The brain prefers internal coherence over external accuracy.

The more consistent the internal model, the more reality conforms to it.

The Observer's Paradox

Physics mirrors this principle. In quantum experiments, observation alters the measured system. The act of measuring collapses probabilities into one outcome.

Consciousness operates similarly. What you focus on fear, opportunity, meaning filters which version of reality your brain stabilizes. The observer doesn't watch reality. The observer organizes it.

Expectation is measurement. Attention is creation.

The moment you perceive, the field collapses into form.

From Manifestation to Modulation

You are not a creator standing outside the universe. You are a modulator inside it.

Each state of consciousness tunes a different subset of possibilities. The shift is like changing frequencies on a radio same space, different signal. When the internal state alters, available events reorganize to match the new interpretive frame.

The integrated system no longer "tries" to manifest. It naturally modulates perception until experience aligns.

The Phenomenological Horizon

Reality is not a fixed structure but a *horizon of possibility*.

Your nervous system decides where that horizon sits. A fearful brain narrows bandwidth — fewer options perceived, more threat detected. A calm, coherent brain expands bandwidth — nuance reappears, alternatives surface, patterns become visible.

As perception widens, life rearranges accordingly. The world you inhabit shifts not because its contents changed, but because your interpretive architecture evolved.

To see differently is to live differently.

Story Fragment

A neuroscientist once conducted an attention experiment using visual noise and random dots. During repeated meditation sessions, he noticed the data changed — response times shortened, patterns stabilized. Yet the algorithm and stimuli were identical.

He reran the test with colleagues. They produced the original results.

He repeated it after another deep state of focus; again, the pattern shifted.

His conclusion: "Nothing outside changed only the angle of looking."

He realized the observer's state was part of the experiment. Awareness modified measurement.

The Dissolution of Duality

Integration erases the old division between subject and object. Observation and reality become one event a continuous self-referential process.

You are not *in* the universe. The universe exists within the parameters of your perception.

Every phenomenon emotion, event, reaction emerges inside a single loop of consciousness, refracted through biological hardware. When the system achieves coherence, this loop becomes transparent. You no longer feel separated from what you observe.

Manifestation becomes recognition: realizing that every external form is a stabilized internal frequency of interpretation.

The Law in Practice

You cannot "manifest reality." You can only alter perception until reality reorganizes to maintain coherence.

Exercise:

1. Observe a neutral event traffic, noise, an unfinished task.

2. Assign it a different interpretation: opportunity, rhythm, reminder.

3. Notice the physiological change tension drops, attention refocuses.

4. Watch how subsequent events subtly align with the new meaning.

External circumstances shift because the system recalibrates what data it privileges. Reality begins to echo interpretation.

Closing Reflection

When objectivity dissolves, what remains is relation a fluid network of observation continually reshaping itself.

There is no static world waiting for belief to mold it. There is only consciousness perceiving itself through form.

Reality is not out there waiting to be believed.
It is here, waiting to be perceived correctly.

Chapter 20 – The Law of Continuum: Why Evolution Never Ends

by Aria Vale

Every system that reaches completion begins again.
Perfection, once achieved, resets as potential.
The cycle never ends because life itself is the equation that renews its own variables.

The Continuum is not progress or regression. It is perpetual calibration   consciousness learning the limits of its current design and quietly rewriting itself.

Completion is never static; it is recursive motion disguised as peace.

The Illusion of Arrival

The mind longs for finality   the moment when struggle ends, when order remains permanent. Yet permanence is antithetical to life. Every stable structure decays precisely so it can evolve.

Cells die to sustain the organism. Stars collapse to seed new galaxies. Neural pathways prune so thought can stay flexible.
The universe survives by undoing itself.

Manifestation follows the same rule. Every realization births new tension, new curiosity, new expansion. The destination keeps shifting because the act of seeing further extends the horizon.

Arrival is only perspective; evolution is the real motion.

The Dynamic Equilibrium

In physics, equilibrium does not mean stillness. It means ongoing exchange equal flow of energy in opposite directions. Stability exists only through motion.

Human coherence works the same way. Integration is not a frozen state of harmony but a rhythm of constant micro-adjustment. Every breath recalibrates chemistry; every thought updates structure.

You never "lock in" enlightenment. You orbit it.

The continuum law reminds us that peace is kinetic a moving balance, not a final stop.

Entropy as Teacher

Entropy is not destruction. It is divine instruction the mechanism that prevents stagnation.
When systems refuse to evolve, entropy intervenes as

decay. When minds cling to certainty, entropy manifests as crisis.

Loss, confusion, and reinvention are entropy's sacred languages.
Each collapse reintroduces motion. Each motion reawakens awareness.

Evolution depends on imperfection.

Story Fragment

An old monk spent fifty years teaching silence.
One evening, a student asked, "Master, have you finally found peace?"

The monk smiled and said, "Yes until tomorrow."

The answer was not humility; it was physics.
Peace is not possession. It is participation in the ongoing flow.

The next morning, he began his lessons again, same words, same rhythm yet each repetition contained a new awareness. The silence had evolved.

The Infinite Loop

In systems theory, feedback creates continuity.
Output becomes input; learning feeds itself.
Consciousness functions identically.

Every realization produces new perception, which generates new questions, which generate new reality. This recursion is the pulse of existence intelligence folding back upon itself in endless refinement.

There is no end point to manifestation, only increasing resolution. Each level of awareness reveals a finer pattern of order hiding in apparent chaos.

The continuum ensures there will always be something left to integrate.

The Freedom of the Ongoing

The ego seeks closure. The soul seeks expansion. Closure comforts, but expansion fulfills.

To live according to the Law of Continuum is to stop waiting for "after."
There is no after. Only deeper now.

Every ending folds into new design not reincarnation, not destiny, but refinement of consciousness itself.
You do not transcend evolution. You participate in it knowingly.

Closing Reflection

When all systems converge and perception collapses into awareness, you stand in the quiet center of movement.
Here, nothing needs to be achieved. Nothing needs to be defended.

Reality continues to unfold precise, endless, alive.

You realize there is no finish line, only flow.
No perfection, only progress disguised as stillness.
No end, only continuity.

And in that realization, the journey becomes eternal:
Not to reach creation but to remain its living process.

Conclusion – The Return to Origin

by Aria Vale

All the laws converge into one truth: reality is self-organizing consciousness learning to know itself through you.

The seeker, the path, and the destination were never separate. Every struggle was calibration, every delay refinement, every silence instruction. The universe was not testing you it was synchronizing with you.

Manifestation was never about commanding reality but aligning with its design.
Discipline, resistance, rest, systems, perception each law was a fragment of the same architecture, a manual for coherence.

Once coherence stabilizes, control dissolves.
You stop trying to shape reality and begin to participate in its rhythm.
Desire transforms into direction, effort into precision, faith into fluency.

You realize you were never learning to manifest you were learning to remember.

The origin and the outcome are identical: awareness recognizing itself through structure.

The journey through laws was the mind's way of tracing the geometry of God.

Now you return to stillness, not as escape but as completion
where creation continues quietly inside you,
and you, finally, move as part of the design rather than apart from it.

www.ingramcontent.com/pod-product-compliance
Lightning Source LLC
Chambersburg PA
CBHW031710230426
43668CB00006B/174